ALWAYS BE HAPPY

ABOUT THE AUTHOR

The author is a trained economist, after working for some years as a financial inspector, she quit her job and chose a humanist path.

Together with her husband, she owns and manages a guesthouse in the mountains. There, she has created a spiritual center, Shanti Spiritual Centre.

She is a Bowen, Reiki, Bach and Yoga therapist. She conducts 'Yoga for Health' class at her hometown's Culture House, in Cluj-Napoca, Romania. There, she has hosted conferences on Indian culture. She also hosts different spiritual courses such as: Happiness Course, Guiding Souls beyond Death Course and Youth Elixir – Immortality Elixir.

She is currently writing spirituality books, both for kids (a series of tales with Angels) and for adults. She has taught Romanian Language at an Indian University.

She coordinates a theatre group, putting on stage mainly spiritual plays written and directed by her. She has been on tour in India several times. Loving spiritual travels, she has visited special places in Europe, Israel, Egypt and India, and written about them.

Her greatest joy is to be of help to others, in every possible way.

ALWAYS BE HAPPY

Semida David

ZORBA BOOKS

ZORBA BOOKS

Published in India by Zorba Books, 2017

Website: www.zorbabooks.com
Email: info@zorbabooks.com

Copyright © Semida David

ISBN Print Book - 978-93-86407-89-4
ISBN eBook - 978-93-86407-90-0

Zorba Books Pvt. Ltd.(opc)
Gurgaon, INDIA

Printed at Repro Knowledgecast Limited, Thane

I dedicate this book to God

ABOUT THE BOOK

This book is an autobiography, recording the author's journey from being a non-believer to a complete devotee of God, spanning over more than twenty-five years of her life.

Raised under the communist regime, the author didn't get any religious education. After the revolution that freed the Romanian people from communism, she happened to attend a yoga course that had recently opened in the country. It was there that she started opening up to spirituality.

Her journey followed two parallel ways: on one side, the yoga classes brought her closer to the spiritual science of the Orient, and on the other side, the genetic heritage came to light, opening her heart to Lord Jesus Christ.

Using the meditative techniques that she learned at the yoga classes, she started to realize long meditations of communion with Jesus, wishing to meet Him every day.

After a few years, India opened its gates and welcomed her with love. This allowed her to discover within the Indian temples, all that she had learned over the years at the yoga classes she attended in Romania.

Fluctuating between Hinduism and the Christian faith, she discovered that she was able to find God in each of them, such that, in her heart, Shiva and Jesus were united as One.

The book also describes fragments of her spiritual journey in India and the spiritual challenges she went through till she discovered God.

This is a book for all, regardless of individual religious beliefs, because as the author says, she meditated in temples, in churches, in mosques and even in the Egyptian pyramids, and everywhere she was able to find God.

It emphasizes on God's love and kindness, considering that, for her, it was an immense grace to see all the patience God has with someone who had rejected Him at first.

Her entire spiritual journey was possible only through God's infinite love and His grace which is, in fact, bestowed upon all of us, without distinction.

PREFACE

I have known God's love and tenderness. Jesus guided me to discover His love and beauty, and now, I pray for the strength to write about all the wonders that have happened in my life, and that can happen in each of our lives…wonders that often happen without us even noticing them.

In each moment of our lives, we are all blessed with God's love and care, and all of us are loved by God equally.

He doesn't differentiate amongst people; it is we who think He does that. We live in duality; we perceive the world as duality, but God is beyond duality and He looks upon each of us in the same way. The Idea that some of us are better than others is our perception, a human perspective. It is not God's view. All it takes is a small step beyond this illusion and you will be able to see the mind games we play that enslave us for lives over lives.

I don't know when I embarked on this spiritual journey, in which of my past lives. I don't know if I can be called a spiritual being. All I know is that in this life I felt a lot of His love and also His guidance. I felt His grace bestowed upon me, although at the age of 22, I did not believe in a higher force, superior to us humans. I wasn't just a non-believer; I vehemently denied the existence of a God. I am ashamed to confess to this, but you must know how I was before. Once, I was in a conversation with someone who was trying to convince me about the existence of God. I ended the talk abruptly and told the person: 'If God exists, then He should strike me with lightning right now!'

A moment of silence followed – terror appeared on the other person's face as I waited for the divine sign. It never came.

God will never play games with us, even when we behave foolishly.

Then something did happen – a revolution. Some say it was in vain, but that's because they look outside themselves and not within their beings.

There was a revolution in my country, which brought changes in all aspects of life, but most of all in human qualities. Looking externally, we can still see the country fighting for 'freedom'. But if each of us gazes into our souls, we would be able to see the big transformation that our spirit has gone through and the great freedom that came forth.

Since then, Romanians became free: free to choose what they believe in, what to do, what to study, where to travel, free to believe in God and to enjoy life.

Two important events then occurred in my life: the first was discovering Jesus and the second was when I met God.

In this book, I have described the life that I've lived till now. A splendid life, a wonderful life, a life filled with the love that God Himself gave to me.

This feeling of plenitude and fulfilment that I experience each day helps me deal with all of life's small problems that come and go like the waves of a mountain river.

As a matter of fact, I started writing this book on many occasions and each time I stopped for the same reason: I was not ready to share it with the public.

I've been on a long journey, from complete ignorance to discovering God, all with the help and guidance of Jesus. I was able to find God closer than I expected.

For over 25 years, I didn't want to talk about this publicly because I didn't want to create a school, a spiritual path, to be a guru or a teacher.

But if I don't do this now, I feel my life will have been in vain.

I owe this to God Himself. Despite my ignorance, He was always kind and good to me and He loved me unconditionally. I also owe this to our kind Jesus who 'invested' in me, worked on my soul, believed in me and took me from the lowest step of consciousness, guiding me towards God.

The easiest way to convey a message is through a book, because the book will travel and get to those that need to read it.

JOURNAL

Now, being in India and visiting the temples and the spiritual places,

I felt that this was the moment to start again, for the last time - in other words, to start writing and not stop until I've finished. I was writing, and simultaneously thinking about the world, which was unsettling - but I wouldn't stop. I kept writing and thus respecting my promise.

Will the people believe what I am telling them? This thought obsessively haunted me. Who am I to speak about something like this?!

But an experience I had here gave me a strong impulse to continue.

I was in a temple in Southern India.

There are many restrictions in the temples of the South; foreigners are not allowed to enter the temples, only Hindus are.

The Indian temples follow a certain architectural design: they have a big courtyard, the main building being in the centre and, on the sides, you will find smaller temples and altars. My husband and I were allowed to enter the courtyard, but not the main temple. We entered with a certain inhibition. Our souls wanted to be there, we believed in Shiva, we were ready to meet God, but the frowning looks of the priests made us uncomfortable. We were not Hindus; thus, our presence was polluting the sacred space.

We arrived in front of a small temple dedicated to Shiva. It was open. Actually, it was a small building and inside it, there was the idol- the Shiva linga. *There was a pedestal in front of the temple on which was placed Nandi, Shiva's vehicle, according to the Hindu tradition. Other sacred objects were also scattered on the pedestal. We wanted to meditate, as we always did in every sacred place we visited. This practice allowed us to feel the energy of the place and often, the presence of God.*

The soil in front of the temple was muddy because of the water used in the ritual so we couldn't find a place to sit for our meditation.

So, we chose a pedestal to meditate on. As soon as we sat there, a monk came up to us and asked us politely if we were Brahmins. We were not. This meant that we were not allowed to sit there, next to Nandi. It was a place reserved only for Brahmins.

Our souls' devotion had nothing to do with the rules of the temple. For us, Shiva was God, we were in His house and all we wanted was to close our eyes and feel His presence.

We had no choice but to kneel in front of the shrine. We closed our eyes and we started our meditation.

*The spiritual field was very powerful, directing our energies towards **Sahasrara**, the Crown Chakra. I felt the instant sublimation of energies and the powerful activation of this chakra, together with a state of transcendence, of eternity, of being home...the place we are all looking for, a place where we can find our peace.*

After a while I moved away to write in my journal. Then we asked permission to take some photographs but we were not allowed. I desperately wanted to capture the image of that Shiva linga, *no matter what, so that it would remind me of what I felt every time I looked at it. So we tried a different method that had previously been successful: we decided to pay for the privilege of taking photographs! The money we offered was accepted, so we had a deal.*

Again, I felt the need to meditate in front of the Shiva linga. *Something was calling me back there.*

I entered into a profound state and at somepoint, I heard:

Waves come and go,
But you remain there eternal and immortal.
Steadfast in front of the waves.
What can they do to you?
Nothing.
They are just waves!

I felt shaken by this message received from **Shiva** *Himself and that was when it dawned on me: that I must write and publish a book. Regardless of what others would say, the eternity that was given to me couldn't be changed. So I felt I must stay firm as a rock, pursuing my goal and fulfilling it.*

I had God's support.

I was encouraged to continue my work, to write this book that will tell you how I meditated in HINDU AND BUDDHIST temples, in churches, in mosques and even in the great Egyptian pyramid. It will tell you about my quest, about visiting different spiritual paths until I was able to feel God and know that He is One and the same for all of us.

I travelled a lot, I searched and meditated in many places.

Sometimes I was allowed to enter, at other times the access was forbidden, but I never judged anyone because they were all protecting their faith and had their reasons to do so.

From nothing I found Faith, the Temple and the Church in my Heart.

I learned to respect each spiritual path, to believe in them all because I saw that God is everywhere. I learned to rejoice in their existence because through this multitude of paths, each person can choose the one that suits them best.

Part I

I AM THE WAY,
THE TRUTH AND THE LIFE

THRESHOLD

For a long time in our life, everything seems very complicated and difficult, but after a time, when the balance tilts beyond a certain point, everything becomes simple and easy.

Before that threshold, we believe that we are the ones who must do everything, and that burden can seem overwhelming. Beyond the threshold, we trust and leave God to fulfil His will and then everything seems easy and beautiful.

But how do I get over that threshold?

Once I've passed over the threshold will I stay there or return?

Every one of us has his or her path and we all get to choose whether we stay or return.

There are several accounts of people going through near-death experiences and returning to share with us where they have been, who they met and how beautiful it all was. They felt so much love that they didn't want to return.

What I am describing is similar to a near-death experience, except that it doesn't involve a physical death: beyond the threshold you don't want to return to what you were and, more than that, God takes you under His care from all points of view. He is the one protecting you, keeping you there, offering you an abundance of gifts, so that when you have it all, when you feel fulfilled, loved and looked after, why would you return?

From very good, from perfect, where else is there to go?

Just give thanks, over and over and over again -constantly expressing your gratitude to God.

I could write incessantly about His love and grace. I could write hundreds of pages about His beauty, His kindness, His sympathy, His forgiveness. If I do so, I would not stop writing for days and nights.

It doesn't matter that I know so little about God. I could write endlessly because I feel continuously embraced by Him, I feel loved and protected by Him.

REVOLUTION

M y spiritual life and my relationship with Jesus began after the revolution. My parents believed in God but because of the communist society and of their unpleasant experiences over the years, they chose not to offer me a religious education and to keep me away from everything related to God.

This was a good thing; it allowed my mind and my spirit to be free and to receive the direct teachings from God Himself. I've seen many people whose parents made them go to church, to respect the orthodox traditions or any other religious traditions and, despite that, they kept a distance from Jesus. I've also seen people on spiritual paths who lost the faith they had in the path they were on, after years of practice. Subsequently they've lost their trust in anything or anyone who tried telling them about God. Being allowed to develop this freedom of spirit was really beneficial for me and later on, you will understand why.

Because my grandparents insisted, I was christened when I was 18 years old, without any prior religious education. My baptism was a meaningless show for me. When the priest asked me to repeat after him, "And I will unite myself with Christ," I perceived the demons' mockery and that shook me. Their mocking laughter frightened me.

During the revolution, when Ceauşescu's fleeing was announced and with that the 'liberation' of the country, I was on the streets. I will continue to say this: it was a liberation for our country, although I am not a politician or a sociologist to have an authorised opinion.

Church bells rang, people danced on the streets, hugging each other in joy. After a night of terror, when shotguns were directed towards the people, in the morning the pavement still had blood on it. I've seen parts of a human brain next to a curbstone overlooked by those who removed the bodies. People were out on the streets again in a mix of fear and hope. The news of the liberation was well received by the people.

I was alone, witnessing the scene. Then I saw a young man making the sign of the cross, kneeling, kissing the ground and thanking God. I found his gesture ridiculous and I asked myself what faith, what force made this young beautiful man act in such a way?!

Even though I couldn't understand it right then, that gesture triggered a change in me. Who was he thankful to? To whom was he so grateful? That was the first time in my life I was witnessing that there can be something beyond our normal physical perception that can lead us to do things that never crossed our minds before.

Many of those people on the streets believed that it was a Divine intervention which liberated the country, but there were also many others without any faith, like wandering sheep.

Even though many are saying now, twenty years after, that the revolution was in vain, I believe it was not. Beyond the freedom that we were waiting for, we all gained a greater freedom - the one of the soul, of the consciousness, of the spirit.

A nation kept in isolation - without the right to know, to be informed, to acknowledge the existence of a God whose power is greater than that of the president of the state - started to be bombarded with information.

The revolution opened the country's borders to missionaries, priests, teachersand speakers who came to tell us about Jesus and God. Different groups, societies, religious and spiritual movements were being created then.

Conferences, symposiums, books, classes, TV shows, radio shows, spiritual movements, trends, faiths -all possible ways were used to help us and invite us to believe.

Even I had to admit that there was something more, although I only believed in my own powers. I thought that it couldn't be possible that all others were foolish and that I was the only bright one!

But my faith was still non-existent and so it remained until I convinced myself.

YOGA

I started my quest. I was attending all the conferences, churches, cults, spiritual movements... A force was making me search and search and search again... until I arrived in a place where they were not talking about God, but about love. The theme of that conference was self-love, an unknown notion to me back then. Everyone in the hall was relaxed, dressed casually, as though they had arrived from a walk or had spent some time at the swimming pool. It was a Saturday afternoon and it seemed as if there was nothing that could stress the attendees.

The speaker was a good-looking young man, confident in what he was speaking about. It was clear that his speech was based on his own experience and not just some theories cobbled together from books.

I asked around to find out what sort of spiritual action this was and I discovered that, immediately after the revolution, a yoga course had been started in the city. Everyone in attendance had enrolled in the yoga course and the speaker was their teacher.

The exotic, oriental spirit and the curiosity for the paranormal made me stay there for a while. For the first time in my life, I was attracted to something spiritual.

For a former communist country, yoga was an open door to freedom and spirituality all together. In all the other places I had visited, the faith in God was imposed and that was not attainable overnight. When you keep telling a soul that is not receptive to believe in God, it becomes annoying and disturbing. Having in mind the number of believers before the revolution and their number today, I say it again, loud and clear, so that all Romanians can hear me - brothers and sisters, the revolution was our rescue! We are born, we live and we die, we have plenty of food and all the products we might wish for. We get hundreds of chances for personal development but our biggest gain, in my opinion, is the freedom of our spirits and the fact that so many Romanians now believe in God.

Coming back to the yoga course,

hey were not talking about God. The focus was on asanas, energies, resonance, love, relaxation…

The person who structured the course was smart. He understood our situation, the way Romanians were after the revolution and he prepared us to discover God ourselves. He did not force us to believe in Him.

After I discovered the divine vibration, the yoga course transformed itself into a deification course.

I followed the classes with joy and pleasure because they were offering me a chance to learn many interesting things. I was building up my spiritual knowledge, learning about oriental and occidental saints and liberated beings, about different spiritual paths, all gathered in one place. There were many young people, the teacher too was young. The environment was relaxed and pleasant in comparison to other places where a certain attire and conduct were required. Yes, there were rules here too, but it felt more like a spiritual celebration than a religion. It didn't become a religion either way, as it was later discovered. We were doing asanas, we were meditating, there were conferences, we were watching spiritual films together - in short, it was a very pleasing atmosphere which suited my needs perfectly.

JESUS

One day, in class, I received a photograph with the image of Jesus as it had appeared on the piece of cloth that was used to wipe His face on His way to Golgotha (how can such a thing be possible?).

I pinned it on the wall but it didn't impress me much. After two months though, something unexpected happened. I was alone in the room, laying relaxed on the bed and at some point, as I was gazing at the picture, suddenly I felt I knew Him. This being who gave His life for us (as it was told) seemed very familiar and from that moment, I started to believe in Jesus. All of a sudden, without any preparation, without any prayer or meditation, without any quest, I started to believe in Him. And my belief was strong. From that moment on, no one could shatter my faith. It was a miracle for my soul. I was astonished, perplexed, but the joy and the flavour of faith made me very happy.

What triggered this change? How did it happen? The asanas and meditations practiced at the yoga course were purifying my subtle body from one week to the next; by participating in the classes and conferences, my soul was slowly opening up. And so, without any constraint to believe in Jesus, my soul was ready at that point; my soul remembered about believing in Him. My soul remembered about believing in Him? Yes, it remembered. In another life, or maybe in more than one, I was a Christian and I had the love for Jesus in my spirit. The faith was brought to light by removing all the coarse subtle bodies. Back then, I didn't understand what had happened, but I was very happy at discovering my soul. But what was I to do with this faith? I was a Christian through birth, christening and faith but never had I been to a priest or to a church, and I had never followed the Christian rituals. I didn't want that and did not feel the need to do so. I knew there must be another method to reach Jesus. But what was that? It was still not clear to me.

I was not praying to Him because I didn't know how to do so. But, because at the yoga course I had learned to meditate, I started to realise frequent meditations of communion with Jesus.

There were so many of those meditations, and they were so frequent, that at some point, I started to hear His mantra. This was a shortcut for connecting with Him – as soon as I sent out the mantra, I was instantly in communion with His spirit.

The more I meditated, the more the longing for Him grew.

And so, I would realise my meditations till one day, when such a longing for Him awoke in my soul. I sat near the bed, on the floor, in a meditation posture, and I told myself I wouldn't get up from there until I saw Him. After a few hours, my first out-of-body experience happened. The sound of the mantra took me deeper and deeper into my heart and because of my commitment to meditate, I started to separate from my physical body and go up and up through each astral sub-plane till I reached a place where I was stopped by a man dressed in white. This was how I perceived Him then. At that time I didn't know much, but later I understood that he was one of God's Angels.

He gently told me:

You can't go further on because you are not ready to meet Him, but know that when you are ready, He will come to you. Also **know that Jesus will come once again and you have to tell this to everybody.** *Now, I will lead you on your way back.*

And saying that, we started our travel back. The Angel led me till the border separating the planes and then I returned to my physical body and I opened my eyes.

This sort of experience can be baffling. When you return, it's like you've just awoken from a dream, but if the experience is real, and not just your imagination, the inner state is modified, the soul recognises the Truth and sooner or later, signs will appear in the physical plane too.

Meeting someone, even though it was not Jesus, was a great joy for me, but the message I was asked to deliver placed me in a difficult situation. First of all, who was I to convey such a message? Who would believe me, when I'd been a non-believer all my life? Secondly, because it was shortly after the revolution, faithlessness prevailed in our country. You could've heard about Jesus' second coming all day long, in every church, cult or on the streets, from the people who wanted to bring you onto their path. I'd heard this message so many times before that it seemed flat. Now, an Angel of God was asking me to deliver it. I knew that this was actually what Jesus wanted from me and this made it even more difficult. Part of me wanted to deliver the message, but the other part didn't know to whom or where. Was I to go to the city centre, stand on a pedestal and shout that Jesus will come once again? People would have said that I am crazy. Or did I have to deliver it at a conference? That would require special preparations; you can't just say something like that and leave. To deliver such an important message, you needed to be a very good speaker and would need to talk about spirituality for at least two hours. But I hadn't read the Bible yet. Plus, I was very shy. In school, when I had to speak in front of the classroom, my face would become red and I would stutter. How could I host a conference? No, it was clear, I couldn't do it.

So, the time passed and I was not completing the mission given to me by Jesus. But I kept meditating daily, till the communion with him became deeper.

In one of the meditations, the following happened: I felt that Jesus was in my heart and from there He was going up, rising towards the sky. Usually I felt Him coming towards me from above, but now I felt Him being born within MY HEART and growing to the sky, where He would unite with God.

Over time, He became my teacher, my master, my guide. Over the next twenty years, He taught me many things, He offered me many gifts and He led me to God.

My longing for Jesus grew deeper and deeper and made me search for Him continuously, with fervour. I used to undertake long meditations in order to reach Him.

I remember one of those meditations that went through different stages.

At that time, my mind was making connections with different, familiar images.

At first, I felt Him calling and there was a determination to start the meditation process. I saw an image from the mountains and a footpath that I was walking on. An obstacle came in my way and I saw myself jumping over it as though it wasn't there. Then, another footpath appeared through the woods; I couldn't see much further in front of me, but I kept walking without thinking about what I would find at the end. I had confidence that I was on the right path. Then a mountain appeared in front of me and I climbed it easily. I got to some sort of a plateau where I received the first sign from Jesus: I felt immersed in a bright white light and a wave of love covered me from all directions. I couldn't walk anymore, I couldn't control my legs. I was just standing there, nourished by that Light as if it were Divine Nectar. I stayed like that for a while, as long as the Grace manifested for me and the Light was pouring over me. Then, as this feeling diluted, I felt in my heart an even stronger impulse to reach Him. This time, I saw myself rock climbing. It was a vertical wall and I was clinging onto the cracks in order to advance, but it didn't feel difficult. In a moment of weakness, I stuck to the wall, feeling that I couldn't go on anymore but even then, I was helped by an invisible hand and I got to the top. Now, for the second time, Jesus gave me a sign: I was again immersed in the bright white light and I felt God's infinite love. The mountain top was so sunny, bathed in so much light, and I was expanding in all four directions as I received the Divine Essence. Again, I stayed in this ecstatic state till it diluted and then I wanted to go further. Honestly, I wanted to arrive in front of Him; to see Him with my spiritual eyes, to kneel in front of Him and to kiss His feet. I looked around and there was nothing there that would take me up any further. Then, I visualised Him in my mind and, like an arrow, I felt I was flying up. With the ease of lightning, I was going through clouds, through the atmosphere, through space, through the worlds... till I reached another vast space where everything was peace and tranquillity. It was similar to a void and it was here that Jesus bestowed His Grace upon me for the third time. Once again, I was immersed in the bright white light and surrounded by love, and I was in ecstasy again. This place's unimaginable peace was impregnating my whole being. I remained in this state until it too diluted and the urge to go further on appeared again. But I couldn't anymore. My energy was consumed. My vital energy? My spiritual energy? I didn't know. All I felt was that all my resources were exhausted.

When I returned from the meditation, the state I had experienced in the last plane kept vibrating in my soul for days.

More than that, I felt I was able to include other people and that I could induce in them the same state I was living in, no matter what my state was, and I was also able to do other things, like controlling their minds and their will. I first noticed that by accident, then I tested it. I noticed that my will was controlling other people's wills into doing different things. Without knowing, they would act in a particular way, doing what I wanted them to. I repeated this experiment a few times, just enough times to assure myself that it was real and to wonder, and then I renounced this ability, preferring to let life surprise me and to respect other people's free will.

In another one of my meditations from that period, when I was devoting my whole being to Him, I told Him that I wanted to be His Bride, like the nuns who never got married. I didn't have any intention of going to a convent - just to live in celibacy for the rest of my life. He answered me then, and I think this was His first direct answer:

THERE IS NO NEED FOR YOU TO DO THIS.

At that time, I believed that celibacy would have been the greatest form of devotion and sacrifice that I was able to offer Him, but He said it was not necessary. My love life hadn't started back then. Now, as I contemplate on that moment, I can comprehend what a great chance it is to integrate love making into your spiritual life.

I am able to say that now, after more than 25 years of spiritual life, because I can see that Jesus was very present and attentive, allowing me to feel His presence in mundane situations. This has helped me to better understand both love and love making.

THE SECOND COMING OF JESUS

Those who see Jesus as just the Son of God, who only came to take away our sins, are terribly wrong: Jesus came and is there continuously to help us with all mundane things, even the most insignificant, because nothing is by chance and everything in our lives has a meaning. Everything is important and has a purpose.

I can't say it with certainty, but isn't this **the second coming of Jesus**?

Can't we consider the proof of this hypothesis that He returned into our lives, that He is right by our side in every step as long as we choose Him and we follow His path? And also, that He is watching over us and gets involved in our lives if we invite Him to?

That image of Jesus knocking at the door isn't far from the truth.

That advice from the priests and our guides on the Christian path, saying that Jesus is knocking at the door of your soul and is waiting for you to open it, even if it is in the last moment of your life -this advice is real. He would enter even during your last moments, and as the Bible says, he enters every house, no matter if the person is good or bad.

So here it is: Jesus doesn't differentiate amongst us. He is at the door of your soul, of each of our souls and waits for us to open it to Him, to let Him enter, to get involved in our lives, to live our lives together with us.

For a long time, I thought that you could address Him for only important things but, with His help, I've seen His joy when He gets involved in seemingly insignificant situations in my life.

But who am I to say what's significant and what is not, when I am still living in duality?

Feeding a stray dog may not be of value for 99% of all humanity, but in the eyes of God, this gesture might be as important as building an orphanage. We see things this way because we live in duality, but God is beyond duality. For Him, each action or gesture has the same importance.

Maybe, from the food that I fed him, the dog will get strength and energy to save a drowning boy two streets away. That is an inspiring scenario, but why not go further? If by feeding a hungry animal, I've opened my heart, maybe that opening of the heart was that which God was wanting from me for years, or maybe lives - an opening that will be the first step towards returning home to Him.

This is the second coming of Jesus. He is already here. He is by our side; we just need to open our eyes and see Him.

If what you are waiting for is a big, shiny Jesus up in the sky, who will come and punish, as some say, who would be a threat, a reason of fear for the sinners and a reason of joy for the good ones, I'm afraid you will act in the same way as those who saw Him two thousand years ago and told Him that they are waiting for the Messiah.

He will return - this was His promise to all of us, all of humanity, not just the Apostles. And just as the Apostles waited for Him, fearful, but with faith, and they welcomed Him and didn't doubt when He returned, it is the same for us now. It would be unjust of Him to promise to return and not keep His word. How long should we wait? What will be the great moment we are waiting for? When will that moment be? Two thousand years have passed and how many others will pass till we all see Him? Either way, there is no written proof to say that there will only be saints when He returns again. It is said that the sinners will burn in hell, which means that whenever He is supposed to return, there will be both good people and sinners.

The moment when Jesus will return is the moment we are ready for Him. He will return for each of us at the right moment. Each one of us has his /her right, favourable moment.

Lately, people are talking a lot about the present moment.

Yes, it's true, the only real moment in time is the present one, but this present time is not a condition for Jesus to return to us. Between our effort to be in the present moment and Jesus' return, there is Grace. And the Divine Grace depends only on the Divine Will.

When the Divine Will manifests, He appears. Actually, He is with us, here and now, with all of us. Just close your physical eyes, open up the eyes of your soul and you'll be able to see Him. Welcome Him into your life, but don't expect Him to take away your sins, because that is not why He came. He will guide you, step by step, in your life. He will teach you, He will explain different things to you, He will show you the way. He is even more accessible than you might imagine.

Yes, when the heart is pure and ready to understand, then will come the moment when He will 'take away your sins' - in other words, Grace will be manifested, burning your karma of suffering. But that will not be done unconditionally. What is needed in return is a cleaning of your soul and pure love.

It seems complex but, in fact, it is simple.

God prompted me to teach a course and it is there that I am explaining this process in more detail, so that it can be easily understood by everyone.

If we think that God will come and His appearance will be as big as the sky, then that's how we will see Him. Each one of us will have a moment when we will see Him, because He will come for each of us. It's up to us how soon we open the eyes of our souls in order to see Him.

That moment will be a milestone in our evolution. From that moment on, we will be different. Something will transform in our beings for eternity.

JOURNAL

*A*s I was writing this book, precisely when I was writing this chapter, I received an unexpected visit from a friend I haven't seen for over thirty years. And as we were talking, flitting from subject to subject, we came to discuss spiritual things. I told her about God and the possibility to simply communicate directly with Him and, in a moment of intimacy and trust, with slight hesitation in her voice, my friend asked me:

- *Did you have visions?*

The reality is that many people have visions but most of them are afraid to talk about them, thinking that these are permitted for only saints.

I then felt her hesitation and, at the same time, her hope that she could tell me about her experiences.

- *'Yes', I answered, encouraging her.*

So she started telling me about her experiences. Once you have such an experience, it will mark you for the rest of your life and, till your relationship with God becomes stable, you'll feel the need to talk about it with someone. Not to confirm it. The Godly Truth beholds in itself the truth, so when your experience is authentic, you need no confirmation from others because you know it was real.

This woman, who I met thirty years ago and with whom I've travelled a lot and is a close friend, had in her youth a certain something that was pleasant and appealing and awakened love.

She was the kind of person that everybody loves, who knew how to be pleasing with an adorable smile that came straight from her heart.

To be honest, she mentioned that even when she was a teenager, she'd had visions of the Virgin Mary and I tell you this, now, as a parenthesis, so you would better understand her experience:

- I was walking on a river bank with my friend, who was pregnant, and my two young daughters, who were then five and two years old. We arrived at a place where there was a statue of the Virgin Mary surrounded by Angels. My daughters said: **Let's pray for daddy!** My husband is a navigator/seaman; he is away for long periods of time and his work is pretty risky. He always said that he can bear to be away from home if he prays to God every moment.

I said a short prayer and I waited in front of the statue for my girls to finish their prayers. I was listening their sweet and pure voices as they uttered sincere prayers for their father. All of a sudden, a feeling of peace and tranquillity came over our souls, without us realising where it appeared from. We stayed there, in front of the Virgin Mary, for a while more, without saying anything. Then we left in silence, only whispering goodbye to my friend. We arrived home, without saying a single word, and when I opened my bedroom door I saw, through the window, in the sky, our Lord Jesus, as big as the sky. It was shocking. I started to tremble and I covered my face. I had never considered myself to be worthy of seeing Him. In those few moments that I saw Him, I was impressed with His beauty, His greatness, His love and kindness. I ran to the girls' bedroom, I took them by their hands and brought them to my room. We kneeled in front of the holy image I had in my room and we started to pray. I was afraid something terrible was about to happen. I prayed for three hours. I was shaking. The girls stayed with me all the time and didn't ask me anything. Only later, was I able to get up and put the girls to bed.

Later, when I was able to talk with my husband, I told him about my experience and he said that right about that time, he could have been injured by a cylinder head that fell exactly where he was working. Without him realising who or how, he felt an invisible hand pulling him away and saving him.

My friend and her daughters didn't know he was in danger, yet they had felt the need to pray for him. That prayer probably saved him.

Once again, at an important moment when writing the book, God sent me a helper.

I will come back to this subject later on; right now I just want to emphasise that if someone is praying for us with all their heart, God will answer their prayer.

The story I just narrated reveals the existence of a superior intelligence that knows and comprises everything. Some call it God (or have other names for it, like Allah, Shiva, Yahweh, etc), others call it the Great Spirit or Consciousness that comprises everything - without acknowledging the affection on His part, only the Law that sustains and makes the Universe function.

Later on, you will get to know my opinion on the above, based on my direct interaction with Him.

Beyond the fact that this Superior Intelligence knows everything, the story above clearly demonstrates that we are connected and, with a small effort on our part, we can communicate empathically and telepathically without any problems.

All we need is a little spiritual practice.

I will digress once more to share with you one of my dreams. Who knows, maybe someone will read this book and will make it come true somewhere on this planet. My dream is to create a Spiritual University, similar to those where students go to study for a career. In this university, there would be courses on empathy, telepathy, astral travels, communications with Angels, spiritual therapies, bardo (the soul's travel after death), the teachings of Jesus, Shiva, Mohammed, Mahavira, Buddha, etc. The teachers would be truly spiritual people, who are not interested in wealth or power, and the exams would be passed based on the spiritual achievements of students and not through bribery.

I am sure that we are not far from establishing this University somewhere.

Now, I will return to the main idea: Jesus is amongst us, ***His second coming is already here*** *and more and more people will be able to see Him and communicate with Him directly, naturally.*

I MET HIM

I continued to meditate and search for Him.
My wish to be in front of Him and to see Him was becoming more and more intense.

After sometime, my soul's wish came true: Jesus started to appear as light on a few occasions and once, I saw Him in human form, dressed in white, walking alone through a deserted area. My joy at finally seeing Him was indescribable! Alone in a deserted area was in fact a symbol – it represented my deserted soul. I was still far from being ready to meet Him.

It took me years, but I finally made it!

At first, it was a calling. Then He taught me an important lesson.

I was out in the city one day. It was winter. All of a sudden, I felt Him calling out to me. I stopped in my tracks, forgot about my plans and searched for the closest church, where I started to meditate. It was cold as the church was not heated and I was shaking but I felt I must remain there for as long as He wished.

After about two hours, I saw Him. With great humbleness, He told me:

Jesus is not how they (the world) *think He is, He is the Son of God, but the people are not seeing Him as He really is."*

I understood the idea that people don't really know what it means when they say that He is the Son of God or even what being the Son of God is. Then Jesus raised His head and looked me in the eye. He was very beautiful and I felt my soul crying. We don't really know who Jesus was or is. There is so much confusion about this. Through generations, a certain type of information about Jesus was transmitted to us. Those who met Him knew Him in all His splendour but then, His story was transmitted from one generation to the next and the emphasis was on His crucifixion. Those who haven't met Him and told us His story, emphasise this moment, presenting Him as a weak man who falls under the burden of the cross, who prays to God for that cup of suffering to pass from Him if that it possible, who dies on the cross as a common man. This is just one episode of His life, but not the one that defines Him. This defines Christianity. People need drama to impress them. If we take away the miracles from the legacy of Jesus, Christianity wouldn't have appeared. The drama of the crucifixion and the miracle of resurrection were the basis for this religion. Jesus chose to realise this, maybe as it is said, to wash away our sins (what happened was a big karmic burning), but that is not what defines Him. Jesus is a very strong spirit and this spirit in a human body made Jesus a very strong man from all points of view. He was not weak, as He was depicted, with a sad, skinny face. He was not spending his time crying over human foolishness. A strong man won't cry at the sight of stupidity, poverty or famine. Jesus had compassion. But which painter or sculptor managed to transmit the compassion of this strong man through his art? For the human mind, compassion is confused with pity and pity is associated with weakness, feebleness (depicted through a thin body), sadness and disappointment.

This is how we see Jesus depicted nowadays. Only Michelangelo had a true vision of Jesus. He painted Him as strong and victorious (maybe a bit too muscular, but that was a characteristic of that period). Maybe there are other artists who felt that Jesus was more than what He was said to be but, unfortunately, most of the time I saw Him in churches, in squares or other places, as being crucified and covered in blood.

Jesus is not like that and that is not the way we should remember Him.

He was a strong being and He is a very strong spirit. Let's remember Him this way, let's imagine Him like this. He had awakened all the qualities of a perfect man and as a spirit, He is the Son of God, completely identified with God Himself. As He himself used to say:

I and the Father are one.

It is easy to imagine how a perfect being, man or woman, endowed with all the divine qualities, would look like.

After this meeting, I felt an inexplicable happiness, freedom, strong emotions, energy, determination and self-confidence. I lived the joy of this first meeting with Him for a few days.

I was floating but I was also confused.

When Jesus said that people don't understand what it means when it is said that He is the Son of God, He meant that the people often forget His power- his real power.

In order to help me understand what humbleness is, He manifested that state and I perceived it through empathy. When a master exemplifies you a state, you live it to the core of your being. It is like he is planting the seed of an archetypal state in your being, which is ready. Afterwards, having the model in you, like a seed planted on fertile land, you begin to learn, to grow to perfection, to mould yourself until that state becomes your way of being. Of course, that happens only if you wish to do so; if not, you can let the chance pass you by and maybe, you'll encounter it again over many existences.

The first lesson was humbleness, a state I needed to awaken if I wanted to really communicate with Him.

Having this example of the state of humbleness, I wanted it to be my way of being. I wished it, but I lacked the means to get to it. I just evoked the example of Jesus and I kept in me this constant wish till I was able to relive it, many years after. I want you to know that the real state of humbleness has nothing to do with our image of being humble. It is not being humiliated. It is not a shame to be humble; it's a chance, an honour.

It is a spiritual state which I wish I could find the words to describe, but I can't. Only the language of the soul can convey it and only those with an awakened soul can feel it. If all that you can achieve in a lifetime is to constantly manifest humbleness, you can say you have evolved significantly.

In a few words, I can tell you that humbleness comprises love, compassion, understanding, obedience, embracing others, offering, sacrifice, joy at being able to help others and many more qualities.

From that moment, I felt that Jesus is always with me and that He helps me in every situation, most often without me even realising it.

I am sure that it's not only Jesus watching over us, but also God.

We receive His love and care every moment but we rarely acknowledge it.

In my life, like in everybody else's, He intervened long before I understood it. After my spiritual life started, I perceived and I recognised some of the experiences but I never dared to think that I would get His attention.

THE YOGI

M y inner life was somewhat separated from the yoga course I was attending. On one side, at the yoga course I was learning many practical spiritual things that I was applying in my daily life and these produced marvellous states. On the other side, there was this communication with Jesus that was going on under His direct guidance. Jesus became my master. I still did not understand many things, but He was guiding me, teaching me, always by my side. I was like a child, walking hand in hand with Jesus as my guide.

After three years, my yoga teacher told me that, in fact, he was not 'the big teacher' of this yoga course. He too had a teacher, the one who actually led this school, and I was advised to meet him.

I agreed and I went to meet the yogi in Bucharest, the place from where all yoga teachings were transmitted to the entire country.

A few days before the meeting, I fell very sick and I thought I would not be able to travel. I felt it was a chance I couldn't miss so I travelled by plane. A train journey would have been too difficult for me given my state.

I went to the hall where the yogi was holding a conference; I attended the whole program and at the end, my teacher presented me to the yogi. He looked at me and told me that he was happy to meet me, and he caressed my face. That was all that happened at that first meeting, but after that caress, my sickness went away instantly. It was an experience that was paranormal and it impressed me. For the first time, I was living such a thing, I was experiencing it... I have read and heard about such stories before, but had never seen or experienced anything similar.

I returned home and, since then, I started paying more attention to the spiritual activities held by the yogi. I also began to participate in some of them. At the same time, my teacher was attentive to me too and there were moments when I felt that he knew everything I was doing. Sometimes, in the night, my teacher would appear in my dreams, telling me what I did wrong during the day and what to pay attention to; that made me trust him even more.

Once, I went to see the yogi and asked him a question about something that was of great interest to me. My desire to reach God was immense and at the yoga course we had started to learn about the Great Cosmic Powers. I was attracted to and fascinated by them. Meanwhile, my relationship with Jesus was direct and beautiful. I didn't know one thing though: who is closer to God - the Cosmic Powers or Jesus?

I decided to meditate with whoever was closest because of my intense desire to reach God in this lifetime.

The yogi answered that after God the Father, then comes the Son, the closest, and only then follow the Cosmic Powers, which were even used by Jesus during His human existence.

It was the answer I was hoping I would hear.

I told the yogi about my love for Jesus and about the message He had asked me to convey related to His second coming. He invited me then to one of his conferences where I could transmit the message. I went for the conference, but there were only a couple of hundred people there, so I had to find other occasions to spread the message.

I continued joyously to meditate with Jesus, which would in turn enable me to receive more teachings from Him.

ASK ME ANYTHING

One day I was home alone, practicing **hatha yoga** and all of a sudden, I heard a strong voice above me saying:

Ask me anything and you shall have it!

I flinched and asked myself who had spoken. Was there someone else in the house? I checked every room but no one was there. Who could it have been?

Twenty years passed before I realised whose voice it was. And that was not because I was stupid; I've had an intuition about it, but my common sense prevented me from believing that I was better than others and that I would receive so much grace.

I was surprised and amazed and for years I told nobody about the episode, convinced that they wouldn't believe me. In fact, till now I haven't spoken about it to anyone.

In spite of that, He kept His promise. I had a life that offered me all that I asked for and also all that I merely manifested an intention towards. There were just two exceptions. These were when, if my desires had been fulfilled, they would have separated me from God. I always felt shrouded with the love and care of the One who loved me from the beginning of my existence, without me even knowing it. He had immense patience and understanding for me, because for years, I didn't know about His existence and when I knew, I denied Him. But He was there with me at all times and He helped me.

I am profoundly grateful to Him for this.

JESUS WAS ALWAYS WITH ME

In the meanwhile, I continued my relationship with Jesus. I evoked Him in meditations and He was by my side, helping me. He was my companion, my friend, my brother, my master, helping me in all of life's situations. He was always assisting me. I learned to trust Him completely and to have faith that He is always watching over me. I remember what happened once, when the company I owned was inspected by the Financial Guard (the Romanian tax control agency). We had moved the company's headquarters to a new address but we didn't update the company's papers to show it. In such situations, the fine imposed is quite big. My only chance was Jesus. I started to meditate and once I felt His presence, I asked Him to help me. After a while, He let me feel that there was no need to pray anymore. Like before, when I asked for His help, He would always let me know when things were sorted. I stopped my prayer-meditation and I was sure that everything would be alright. After an hour, my accountant rang me and told me in amazement:

I don't know what you did, but the controllers forgave you. I've never seen that happening before!

I used the same method for other situations because that's how life is. Sometimes it was karma, other times it was negligence and both these got me into situations where I needed help.

Another time, I became ill. The doctors suggested emergency treatment. I didn't want to go through that; I wanted to pray and follow natural treatment. So, I signed a declaration refusing the prescribed treatment. I signed it knowing that Jesus would help me, despite the doctors telling me that I would die if I didn't start the treatment immediately. I admit I was a bit nervous…

My heart was continuously praying.

It was not long before Jesus came (in the subtle plane) and told me:

I will help you this time too, but don't continue like this anymore!

This time, thetone of His voice was harsh, like a parent to his child when the child has done something wrong.

I then saw His angry face and I imagine that it must have been the same when, at the temple, He overturned the tables and drove out those who were selling and buying there.

He was right. A human life comprises many events, many choices and I had made mistakes. It was right that I shouldn't continue as before.

I healed instantly. Jesus kept His promise and so did I, stopping the lifestyle that made me sick.

There are many other examples I can give you, other life situations that He sorted out for me - some of them simple, others complicated. I was like a child getting into trouble, asking for help and receiving it every time.

After a few years, I allowed myself to step into the fascinating world of the Cosmic Powers. I was led away and I started to meditate more with them; Jesus was now in second place. My life became more difficult. The Cosmic Powers were not close to me; they were unable to help me through all my life experiences. So suffering appeared in my life.

One day, a good friend came by and told me she had a message for me, from Jesus:

Today, when I made a blessing for you, I saw you in a round room that had six pillars; in front of each pillar was a person.

You were in the middle, surrounded by a light tube coming down on you from the top without end. A seventh person was watching over you. Six rays of bright white light intensified level with your heart. All of a sudden, you fell to the ground, crying. An intense light appeared in front of you and took the form of Jesus. He lifted you, embraced you and asked you:

Why are you crying my child, when I always love you and embrace you?

You looked at Him and then you kissed His feet, flooding them with your tears. He knelt next to you. You were both kneeling in front of each other and at that moment, He sent a bright white light from His heart to your heart. The intense ray of light grew until it became a light sphere and you melted completely in the heart of Jesus.

This dear friend received this message for me, without knowing about the relationship that I had with Jesus, because, as I said before, I was keeping my experiences a secret.

That made me aware of the huge mistake I had made by placing Jesus in second place. Who knew for how many lives I had prayed and offered myself to Him? Now, when He was always by my side, I had forgotten Him.

I renewed my relationship with Him then and never abandoned it again.

His help, His protection, the meetings with Him, His constant love, understanding and forgiveness awakened in me a great love for people, for the world. The love I felt for the world was so powerful and unconditional that I wished I could offer my whole being to it. I often cried at the feeling of such immense love in my heart.

SAMADHI

A new stage, more fruitful, followed in my relationship with Him. He was always present, offering me gifts.

The states I experienced were very special.

When I was in *Samadhi,* I felt God and I was living in that other worldly bliss that you read about in books.

Jesus helped me feel God.

Often, the states appeared outside of meditations, in everyday situations. The first occurred when I was visiting someone who was sick. It was not something serious, just a cold, but it awakened in me a state of compassion that led me to something more. I started to feel the divine calling, slowly at first, then much more strongly. Its intensity grew until I felt I couldn't resist it anymore. I went out on the street and I started running towards God. But then 'towards' transformed into 'through'. Gradually, everything became God: my friends, the furniture, the air I was breathing, the people, the cars. I felt God penetrating my whole being, all my cells, all my pores. I was becoming God myself. Inside and outside we were One, the Same Divine Being. I was not alone, He was with me, so present! He was in me, with me and in everything that I met on my way. He was in the houses, in the trees, He was holding my hand and embracing me from my inner being. He was in the space I was going through; I was walking through Him.

I was running on the street, simultaneously experiencing all these feelings. I was running, feeling that my body was disintegrating. I didn't know what to do with it, how to maintain contact with it. I had no control over my physical body.

I arrived at a church and went in. The evening service had just begun. There were many people inside, including the priest and the choir. Looking at them I felt as though, simultaneously, I was above them as well as a part of them.

I stayed there till the end of the service, experiencing ecstasy.

I watched a woman kissing the image of the Jesus and I felt I was the one kissing it.

Then I watched another person and felt that I was that person too. And then again, I experienced the same feeling, of living through other people, including the priest and the choristers.

I asked myself whether it was possible to be in all of them at once and then, I was in all of them simultaneously.

My being comprised the whole church, everybody…it was boundless.

The church songs that day were different from other times and captured my attention. The sound was coming from everywhere. I looked at the young men singing and I saw it clearly - God was singing through them. God, who was everywhere – in the columns, in the altar, in the people, in the walls, in the paintings, in everything that existed- and was pouring His Grace over us through the music.

It seemed unbelievable, but it was true: the sound spread over us from everywhere, like an avalanche.

After a while, I observed the movement and without realising it, the service ended and the church emptied. The people left with God in them and yet the church was still filled with Him.

I too left the church, stood on the steps and looked around: all I could see was God. He was immense. He was infinite, boundless! He filled the air, the emptiness we believe exists between things.

I took a step and I felt Him heavy; denser than the air. It was like I had to create space for myself through Him, in order to advance.

It was already dark outside and I was walking home. I could not feel my physical body. All sensations of hurt, tiredness, hunger and thirst were gone. It felt as though I was floating over the ground. I was spirit, pure essence and no longer my physical body.

I was looking at the people on the street walking towards me and it felt like I was going through them – I was coming towards me. I looked up at a window and I felt I was there.

Whilst at a bus stop I looked at a tree and felt its sap flowing through me. I became the tree. I was feeling its life in me. I was seeing God as being that tree. God, I and the tree were one.

I experienced this state of communion with God for hours.

After this experience, I knew that God is in everything and everything that exists is God.

Once, I was working at my desk, entering datainto a spreadsheet. While I was working, the Divine Light filled me and I had to stop because I felt I was dissolving into God.

Another time, late in the evening, I had a lot of paperwork to do (I was working as a financial controller back then) and I was very tired. Like Divine Help or a reward for my effort and devotion, the Divine Light filled me then and I experienced the ecstatic state. The tiredness disappeared immediately and I was completely renewed.

The repetition of these states made me realise the connection between the perfect state of the physical body and the *Samadhi* state.

When you are in *Samadhi*, you are in communion with God. God is perfect, so you experience perfection in every aspect.

The state repeated itself many times and I managed to figure out how to get there at will. So once, when I had a cold, in order to get rid of it, I evoked a *Samadhi* state. I felt myself embraced by God and the cold was healed instantly.

Through God's Will, no serious illness has affected me in this lifetime. Whenever something did appear – because of my wrong actions or my existing karma – with God's help, I was cured instantly.

I always tell my patients (because I am a therapist): the more you are in communion with God, the healthier you will be.

All sickness has a cause and that is the absence of God from our lives.

This also explains the concept of miraculous healings: people open their soul to God. Once God is in their soul, the illness is gone. God is never sick.

Another time, I was asleep and I felt the *Samadhi* state approaching me. I entered this state whilst sleeping. I then woke up and I continued to experience it for a while more.

All my experiences led me to a conclusion: the states of communion with God arrive when He decides, no matter how long we meditate, pray or follow any type of spiritual practice.

And if your soul is honest enough and you love God, these states will come to you frequently.

ANANDA

A nd still God was unknown to me.
I was getting closer to Him, without even knowing it, through my yoga practice and the meditations of communion with Jesus that I was doing alone at home.

God was present in my life but my mind had no definition for Him. He was helping me, protecting me and offering me gifts.

I don't know when this closeness to Him appeared, this yearning to reach Him. It was a gradual transformation of my consciousness and Jesus played an important part in it.

A precious gift He offered me was a state of bliss *(Ananda)*. I experienced it for about three months. I don't know the exact number of days, because I didn't record it in my calendar, but it felt like three months. I don't remember realising anything special in order to deserve it. All I can say is that it was God's Will.

One day it came and since then I was in ecstasy, bliss. It was an aromatic happiness that made me feel God and His gentleness through every cell of my being. I felt embraced and caressed by Him at all times. My physical body dissolved into the subtle one and I felt boundless. There was a very special emotion that I felt through every cell. It's difficult to put in words something that is ineffable. All I can say is that in every moment, I felt I was united with Him, caressed and embraced by Him.

I was living my life, with all its daily chores, in this state. I perceived the world differently, as though I was floating. I was moving slower and there were many times when I would stop and stay still for who knows how long. God chose a time in my life when I didn't have a job and no one asked for my help with anything. I had no obligations. All my work and all that I was doing was because of my common sense and my desire to help others.

After about two and a half months, the state occasionally started to dim. I didn't know what to do to bring it back because, as I said, I had done nothing to attain it. One day, I felt tired and I slept. When I awoke, the state had returned. Then I made the connection: I realised that in my sleep, I was going to a place where I could connect with it. So, whenever I felt it was going away, I would sleep, thinking about the state I yearned for. The state would return even after a sleep as short as a few minutes, and then it would stay for a few days. Who knows to which astral paradise my soul was going to recharge, or maybe it was the Kingdom of God?! When I realised it worked, I applied the 'method' whenever it was necessary. Unfortunately, the necessity became more and more frequent, till the state finally disappeared. As I said, it was a gift from God – three months of grace.

This state of communion came together with another gift, a material one this time.

I often say that these states are imaginary if they happened only in the mind, but if they materialise through something physical - a healing, a miracle, a touch of Grace - then we can say that they are real. Till then, the materialisation appeared only in my personal life (where it was seen by those close to me) or, some of them, in the spiritual theatre I was part of.

I will digress and touch upon an incident briefly. I was conducting a theatre and through our plays, the public felt God, Jesusand the Angels. Because of how the play was directed, owing to the soundtrack or of certain evocations made in the play, at the end or during some special moments, the audience would open their hearts and would feel the Divine.

And now, returning to the blissful state – shortly after it ended, our business started to flourish unexpectedly. It was like money was pouring from the sky.

Until that point, my husband and I had either lived with our parents or in rented accommodation. We had never owned a house. But now, with the money coming our way, we managed to save and we could buy our first house. Then we bought a bigger one and we started growing on the material plane too. This manifestation of Grace in the physical plane lasted for over ten years. For me, it was amazing, especially because I instantly made the correlation: by being in communion with God, He was manifesting His grace in all of life's aspects. It is surprising, but if you want to have money, you need to give all of you to God and He will give you everything you need, including money. It was a direct exemplification of a state of plenitude, springing from a complete communion with God which reverberates in the physical world. Till then, we had lived like normal people, planning our expenditures from one pay check to the next. But, immediately after the blissful state, we forgot what it was to worry about the next day. It felt like God had assigned an army of Angels to work for us. The contacts were easily created, opportunities came towards us; everything was flowing and so did the money.

This was an important lesson for me to understand the connection between spiritual fulfilment and material accomplishment.

It was a clear lesson: if you want everything in the physical plane to be in order, all you need to do is to be in a profound relationship with God and He will take care of everything in unexpected ways. Your love and dedication to God is enough; that will bring you all that you need. All our efforts to earn money and survive in this world could be transformed in the joy of loving God.

It seemed as though I had discovered a magical lamp that fulfils all your wishes. Nothing else was necessary other than loving God with all your being.

This whole world is nothing but a Divine gift and Grace. We can receive all we wish, as long as we offer our love in return. I don't know when I started to love God. I don't even know if I loved Him back then. Maybe I was not aware of it. More love was coming from Him towards me, but I was not able to recognise Him so I felt all the love was coming from the heart of Jesus.

When I say that all is Grace, it's because I haven't done anything special to deserve all this. It was His will, His Gift, His Grace. I was like a child, receiving the gifts without knowing why they came. And it's not just me, all of us are receiving these gifts. We all live in this outpouring of Grace and Divine gifts. God doesn't show any difference. He loves us equally and bestows His Grace upon all of us.

What followed was a very abundant period, when my husband and I enjoyed everything we could wish for in this physical plane. We didn't amplify our desires, keeping everything simple and not going to extremes. We enjoyed life, we travelled, we bought useful things and books. We built a guest house, we donated, we started a new business aiming to help others. We even wanted to build a spiritual centre where people would be soaked with everything that might bring them closer to God!

At the same time, we learned - we followed courses, we became therapists, we opened a place where we practiced - all with the sincere desire to help others as much as possible.

I started to write children's stories about Angels, thinking that if the child learned early in life that Angels exist and that they can be called, this would help them later in their lives.

I was given an opportunity to visit India. The material abundance came together with a guidance towards the mysterious and exotic India, which had a part in my story too. Nothing happens by chance. New horizons became visible once the opportunity to visit India appeared.

THE THERAPIST STATE

Meanwhile, Grace was pouring on me in new ways.
One evening, while I was meditating, I had a vision: I was a crippled man, weak, who couldn't use his legs. I suffered from a sort of paralysis. Two other men were taking me to Jesus, to heal me. I was hopeful and I had faith. He was in an orchard and many people were gathered around Him. When He saw us, He turned towards us, waiting for us to arrive before Him. As we approached Him, I saw that we had entered into His aura, which was visible to me. It was bright white, pure and radiated out onto a very large area from His body. The healing process started as soon as I entered His aura and by the time I arrived a few metres in front of Him, I was already able to walk on my own feet. He was looking at me. His eyes were clear blue, spreading love and compassion. I felt His perfect purity and endless love. That was a new lesson for me: I felt that this was the way He healed – the people that He wanted to heal were cured instantly by entering His pure and loving aura. I can't describe this state of perfect purity and endless love, but I felt that by having these qualities everyone would be able to help, to cure others. The meeting with Him was overwhelming and the moment when our eyes met was unique. It felt like He was absorbing me into His being. My mind stopped. I had no thoughts. I was just there, in the present. I will never forget that meeting, that look, that communication. He didn't say anything, but His eyes told me everything. He entered me and

I melted into Him. I was deeply grateful, completely devoted and full of love.

Wishing to become a therapist, this exemplification arrived at the perfect time. I understood then, what complete purity and unconditional love are. I'm aware I still have a lot of work to do on myself till I can manifest these qualities. Understanding appears in the consciousness, not in the mind. You can say you understand only when the experience reaches your spirit.

History has offered us many examples of miraculous healings, following ardent prayers, even for incurable cases. And still, there are some people whothink they don't deserve this kind of grace, that they are sinners and they deserve to suffer and to die. It is very wrong to think in such a way. All of us deserve and are entitled to His love, grace and kindness. He helps all of us, if we ask Him. It is so simple! Just ask Him, just pray! We have equal rights, we are all equal in His eyes. His love is not divided. It is equal, just as the rays of the sun bring light equally to the good man and the bad man.

I CREATED THIS WORLD

Once I was talking with a friend about God, about different realms, universes and how the world we live in was created. That made me think. I admit, I was also a bit upset with God for creating the world and still remaining hidden. To me, it only seemed fair that He should reveal Himself because every human being in this world yearns to see his Creator. (Oh! It was so childish of me to say that!)

JOURNAL

*A*s I arrived at this point of my story, I stopped writing because I wasn't feeling ready to continue. What follows is something very special. It is the description of one of the most important states I've experienced in this life, one when I had the vision of the Divine Light. In order to write about it, I felt I needed to see the Light again.

I started writing this book during one of my trips to India.

Once I reached this chapter, I put the manuscript aside and continued my travel, waiting for the right moment, in order to continue. A few days passed.

One days, I was on a houseboat in Kerala, enjoying the wonderful experience – the scenery, the services, everything was sublime. The holiday seemed perfect.

Our trip onthe houseboat ended the next day, a few hours earlier than expected. We had some free time. It was Sunday, a day of fasting for me. I thought it would be nice to go to a church and meditate there so we asked the driver to take us to the nearest church. Our touristy clothes were totally inappropriate for the church and the Sunday Mass. When you are on a holiday, you lose track of the days, not knowing which day it is. As we entered the church, we saw the congregation wearing their Sunday best and we realised that we were not dressed properly for church. But their emotions, their purity and their devotion kept us there. They looked uponus as their guests, smiling at us and trying to make us feel comfortable.

In India, most of the people are Hindu, so you won't find many Christian churches. Maybe that was the reason whythe Christians were so humble and modest. And when I say that, I mean as an inner state and not their material one. The people we met in church were waiting for the Mass with such a special emotion, as if they were there to meet Jesus Himself. I've rarely seen such an attitude from church going people.

Initially we sat in the first row, but then, since the local Christians dressed in their best were coming for the Mass, we went towards the back of the church, embarrassed by our clothing.

The Mass started; it was in Malayalam, the local language, so we couldn't understand anything. Consequently, we started filming, wanting to have a spiritual souvenir from Kerala. We were amused by what seemed to be the fastest language in the world. The priest was speaking so rapidly it appeared as though he was not breathing.

Beyond the clothes, the language and other exterior aspects, their purity and emotion created a very special state that embraced us.

At some point, I felt I had to surrender my ego and offer everything I had.

I remembered the driver had asked us to pray for him when we entered.

I didn't know his problems, so I consecrated my prayers and my participation to the Mass for him. This detachment and the context that was created, enabled all of us to receive a wonderful gift.

As my adoration for Jesus deepened, I suddenly felt I had to take a picture. I stopped filming, took out my camera and pressed the trigger button. I felt the need to see the picture immediately, and when I looked, I was thrilled: the picture showed a Light that covered the whole church – the Light of the Holy Spirit pouring onto the devotees. The Grace manifested at that moment being a gift for this church, for the people and for me, was the inspiration for me to continue to write. It was exactly what I needed, what I was expecting.

I took some more pictures, but they were normal. We wondered if there had been a photographical error, an overexposed picture or something similar, so we checked the photographical parameters. Nothing had changed so, technically, everything was the same for the pictures before and the ones after. It was just the Divine that was captured in this picture.

As a proof of His Grace, Gods allows us sometimes to see His Light.

And not by coincidence, I would say, a relic, a piece of the Holy Cross, was preserved in this church. After the Mass, the priest came to us and with great humbleness showed us where the piece from our Saviour's Cross was placed.

When we had decided to go to a church, we'd had no specific purpose. We had just wanted to fill our spare time and be in the shade and not outside, in the burning sun. But the Divine Will guided us to this Holy place and allowed us to see the Light.

This 'happening' prepared me for the next narration:

I had a deep and sincere desire to know the One who created this world. That had always been on my mind and my soul was praying to discover Him.

I was alone, my mind absorbed by the Creator.

At some point, I had a vision: Jesus appeared in front of me, surrounded by a dazzling Light. A Light different than any I had seen before. He emanated immense love. It was the first time in my life I was feeling such love. It was bigger than the sum of all the love I had felt in all the states I had ever experienced. I was feeling His tremendous love for the whole world, for everything, even the most insignificant thing that ever existed. He was radiating Love and Light. The intense feeling stunned me in front of Him. I was stone-still. This Love and Light were flowing through me as if I was not there. His vision was of an unparalleled brightness and magnificence.

Smiling, with a gentle and warm voice, He then told me:

I CREATED THIS WORLD

I felt this truth penetrating my being to its core and I had a partial view of the world through His eyes. I was overwhelmed... I was seeing the world and I felt the love which created it. I felt it was created from His overflowing love. Everything around me seemed sacred, every little thing was like gold and diamonds, too precious to be touched by my impure hands or to be walked on by my unclean feet. All was holy. I was looking around me with amazement, gazing on every little thing and not willing to touch it. I had no wish to walk because my steps would be on His Creation.

Everything was Sacred, everything was Holy.

Honestly, till then, I never imagined that this world, this marvellous world in which we live, was created by Jesus.

An embarrassed thought crossed my mind: My Lord, I love you so much and I never knew that you created everything and I even stood up against you. And now, you answer me with so much love!

I had rebelled and now He was pouring all His love over me... I was living the surprise and fascination of this new world that I was able to see and of the immense love that is difficult to describe. Suddenly, the way I saw the world changed. Gratefully, I was crying, I was crying because of all the love,

I was crying with joy and happiness. I was kneeling in front of Him, totally abandoning myself to His will. He was everything and I had never known it, never imagined it.

This whole world is actually His Loving Being.

I was one with His being and the world. At that point, I understood the world and my foolishness from the past. He was love, and so was the world - it was nothing but love. How could I explain this great love? How could I describe this love we are living in?

A Cosmic Ocean of Love.

Everything, no matter how small and insignificant, was created through His immense Love and comprises His love. Even a grain of sand comprises all of Jesus' love.

Thus it was revealed to me - the value of each object. I realised how precious everything is because it includes all His love. I saw the Beauty of every little thing. Even a meaningless flower, a blade of grass had, for me, the brightness of a diamond.

I saw all the love of Jesus around and inside me.

All beings contain the love of God. They were created out of pure love. This world was not created out of earth or clay, but out of Love.

For days, I felt this amazement. The sacredness and holiness were everywhere, reflecting God's image. The love I felt was springing from everywhere, from everything that existed.

I was living in a holy world. We all are.

JESUS ANSWERS US

Jesus was always present in my life.

My relationship with Him deepened. Now He answered each of my questions, attended to each of my needs. I had a direct communication with Him and He helped me whenever I asked for help.

I received numerous ecstatic states as a gift from Jesus.

It took me over twenty years to be really able to communicate with Him. I would consult Him on every aspect of my life and He would involve Himself in it.

We were raised thinking that we need to address Him piously, with reverence. He would not answer every request so we need to ask for His help only in difficult times, not bothering Him with every little thing… True prayer is free from requests… that's what most of us believe.

But He is always in our lives, every minute of it, so if we ask for His guidance in every situation, it will be even better for us. It will be proof that we are with Him also and not just that He is with us.

He can be with each of us in every minute, and He is.

It's beyond our comprehension to understand the immensity of His Being and of His Love. We know nothing about Him, except what there is in the Bible, and even that too is very little.

He taught me that He treats all of us in the same way, with the same love and care. The way we perceive this depends on how much we open our souls.

It's fascinating and amazing to be able to feel Him being with you, all the time.

All we need to do is to believe that He is always with us. His wish is to offer us many gifts and an infinite amount of love. We are unaware of this, but we only need to feel His love once in order to understand that He craves to offer us an abundance of gifts and wants us to always be very happy.

A NEW LIFE

When we have a mission, it is best to complete it without deviating from it. It is said that those who drift away are taken from this world.

As I got close to Jesus, an assay came for me and I failed. Jesus was granting my every wish, offering me all I needed and even more.

I had the wrong attitude towards this outpouring.

I started to give far greater importance to the material world. I was becoming attached to the gifts I was receiving. All came from Him, but I forgot that those were just for my use, and not really mine.

I then had a shocking experience that taught me a lot.

I started to hear the Angels Choir, especially when I was alone. Then I heard the Angel Trumpets, like a calling, like my time was up.

And then it happened. I had a terrible car accident on Christmas Eve. I remember that back then I had drifted apart from my parents, from my friends; I had become selfish and unconscious.

It was a foggy night (as a symbol for not seeing things clearly) and the car I was in, collided with a stationary truck at 80 km/h. I could see the imminent collision and I tried to warn the driver, but he didn't hear me. A strong boom, the car overturned and drifted on the road. It was dark. I lost consciousness.

Something happened there. What I now describe are the events that occurred before that point.

Two weeks before the accident, a group of friends, noticing the coldness of my soul, felt that I was not in a good place spiritually and started to pray for me.

The day before the accident, several friends had strange dreams about me. One dreamt about me as she had dreamt about another friend who had subsequently died the following day. Another had a dream of me going up into the sky, surrounded by Angels. Another friend dreamt that I had gone and I couldn't be found anymore.

All these incidents made me think that I should have left this world then, but, I believe that my friends' loving prayers influenced God to give me one more chance.

I returned from the darkness and walked away from the crash site. The driver had wounds on his forehead that were bleeding, superficial ones, but he was taken to hospital by ambulance. I remained by the overturned car in the middle of the road. It was a Toyota Land Cruiser that was so seriously damaged that it couldn't be repaired.

I was also experiencing great pain in my chest. Of course, it was not just by accident. It was an intense burning of karma at the level of my heart. I was alone in the middle of the road. Nobody was paying attention to me, as I wasn't paying attention to others till then. I rang a specialist company to come and recover the damaged car and then I tried to find a car to take me out of there.

A lorry stopped. It was high and I had difficulty getting into the cab because I couldn't raise my arm to grasp anything. I thought a medical check-up would be necessary so I asked the driver to take me to the emergency room. He left me close by, because the hospital was not on his way. The doctors were amazed when they saw me alone, coming from an accident that had happened thirty kilometres away. I was not aware of how serious my condition was. I had an X-ray and it showed that my sternum was fractured and the bones had moved to the inside, stopping millimetres away from my lungs. I was lucky that the bones hadn't perforated my lungs.

There was nothing they could do in such cases. There was no need for a cast, so they kept me under observation for the night (it was Christmas Eve, as I mentioned before) and the next day they released me.

I had made a mistake again and once more I was saved. It was not by coincidence that the accident happened when Christians celebrate the birth of Jesus.

Jesus offered me everything, He fulfilled all my wishes, but I had become arrogant and profiteering.

I was painfully reborn on the day we celebrate the birth of Christ.

The following period was agonising. The broken sternum was really painful and there was nothing that could be done. The impact left me with a pain in my neck also. I couldn't lie on the bed so I used an ironing table placed ata 45-degree angle to support my back. I understood then the importance of the sternum (and of the heart) in all of our actions. I was not able to grasp even a glass of water because of the pain. I couldn't hold anything in my hand. Every movement in the body was connected to the sternum and I would feel it in that area.

I realised it was a big karmic burning so I used candles for help, as an offering. I started to light 100 candles daily and after a week, the pain in the neck was gone. But the pain in my chest stayed with me till the bone healed.

Those months, till the bone and my soul cured, gave me the time to meditate and understand my wrong actions.

And how many times I asked for forgiveness! How many times I promised I wouldn't do wrong again! But have I kept my word?

Exactly forty-nine days after the accident, we found the same type of car, with similar features, even better I might say, and at the best price. That coincided with the moment when I finished the second *tapas* consisting of lighting the candles.

That was proof that the accident happened out of an affective and spiritual karma, and not a material one.

It was all clear now. I had misunderstood all the love and help that Jesus had offered me.

My chest pain helped me become aware of many things. It was a total reset. I left the material part to be on a secondary plane. The lesson God had given me was that He will offer us all we wish for and even more, but if we have a spiritual mission, that must be fulfilled immediately. I had postponed it for so long! I had even quit it.

Now, looking back, I see how clumsy I was! It was so difficult for me to understand certain things!

But, oh, my Lord, how much you helped me and how much patience you had with me!

You forgave me every time and you loved me just as much.

I was attached to my house and the curtains I had carefully chosen. I remember how proud I was for choosing such beautiful curtains for the house. I despaired at the thought that I might die and wouldn't be able to see them again.

The problem was not the house or the curtains. It was in my attitude towards them, my attachment to them, the deviation from what I had to do in this life.

When you discover God, the attachment to a house disappears because you're at home wherever you are. You are always with God, so you are at home in every place on this planet or in the Universe.

This is the illusion of the material world - we believe it belongs to us, we believe we own it.

But we don't even own our own body. We received it to use whilst on earth and we leave it when we leave this world.

What happens when we die? We leave, taking nothing with us. But if you are really able to feel God in your Heart, all the goods, all the material items are where you are.

Life's lessons are not as they seem: the lesson of detachment, the lesson of love, the lesson of humbleness, the lesson of mercy, etc. The one and only lesson we need to learn is the lesson of becoming one with God, becoming God. We need to understand that God is with us and in us, here and now. God is everything.

If you are poor, always remember God, if you are rich, always remember God. If you are successful, always remember God. Always remember God if you are sick or if you are happy and so on. God is everything and all there is; everything is done through His Will.

I will come back to this notion of Divine Will in a later chapter.

If there were 28765489000 states, situations, feelings, cases, etc in the Human Universe, do we have to learn them all? No. We are made in the resemblance of God. What is above is just the same as what is below, so...we know everything. Remembering Godliness allows us to instantly remember all the life lessons we believe we need to learn. If you found God in one thing or situation, He is in all things and situations. It is not necessary for you to search for Him and find Him in all. If, after only three lessons, we learn to become One with God, all other lessons will be learnt instantly. There is no need to return, reincarnated, just to learn these other lessons. The fact that we think we need to do this is an illusion. Reincarnation happens because of the law of cause and effect, but not to learn lessons.

I learned detachment from material things owing to that accident. But there was still a lot of fog in my head.

The magical lamp I was so happy about earlier was still there. God was not changing His mind, He was not punishing me. But I didn't know how to use it anymore.

THE IDEAL LOVER

Gradually, things returned to normal and my relationship with Jesus regained its fulfilling beauty. Together with my body, my soul healed too.

I was meditating, praying, communicating and He was there, always helping me with everything.

I was still able to attain with ease all I that wanted in all aspects of my life.

A new lesson came, the most important one - the lesson of love. I was loving Jesus and He loved me. But it was just a fraction of what love really can be.

As I said before, life's lessons are not about learning one thing or the other. All that might be named a life lesson has to do with God and not with our weaknesses. We are here to discover God in every situation. We are here to find Him and to remember that we are one with Him, always.

I felt there was more to it, so I asked for more. In love, I wanted everything. And I asked for everything. But never had I thought that I could experience such complete love with Jesus. Believing that, and without realising what I was doing, I was sharing my love between Him and another person from the physical world. But Jesus always said:

If you love your father or mother or brothers more than you love Me, you are not loving me at all.

I loved, but I was mixing my love, I was confusing it. Jesus had His part in my soul; the earthly love had a different part and I was happy because nobody was more loving than I was.

But I didn't understand what love was, so I almost lost everything. Again.

Jesus and God offer their complete help. They love unconditionally, they offer everything, but in your relationship with the Divine, you need to understand the rules. If you don't act properly, you are left aside. But God is not lost; He is patiently waiting for you to return to the right path. But till you discover the right path…oh, the loops you go through, the detours, the lost time, etc.

Such a loop appeared in front of me and I stepped on it with enthusiasm, believing I wason the right path.

I loved; I was floating in an ocean of love, but my consciousness was in the physical world and not with God. My love had conditions.

Just when I thought that everything wasperfect in my life, my earthly love disappeared. All of a sudden, without notice. As I looked around, the world seemed deserted. There was no other person in this world to whom I could offer my love. Not even one, because I had directed all my love to just one person. And that person had left.

I realised then how I had mixed up and messed up the concept of love. How I was unable to be happy with just the love of Jesus, needing an earthly love.

It felt like universes collided and I was caught in the middle. I was crushed. I had tons of love in my heart and I didn't know what to do with it. My heart was bursting withlove and I didn't know how to offer it and to whom.

My soul ached. What was I to do? How would I survive from now on? Why hadhe gone? I had offered him all my love, and the love reserved forJesus also… I had given him all my love, he had everything, why washe gone then?

My mind collapsed.

Part of me loved Jesus and the other part had the earthly love and I didn't know what to do with it. I was torn.

After about two months, I said to myself: *I cannot go on like this anymore. If my love is not well received here, on earth, then I will send it to the Heavens.*

In the two months that followed, all the love I felt, I directed towards Jesus.

I was meditating and praying continuously to Jesus. I was offering my whole being to Him, not just all my love. I would do thisday and night. But I felt it was not enough. So I prayed even more, longer, better and I would offer myself more too.

I received what I asked for at the right time.

I was praying and at the same time I was asking Him to let me know the ideal love, the one which replenishes your soul completely and will never harm you.

I was meditating, I was there with all my being, full of love and abnegation, as I had donein the past months. I was not torn anymore.

Jesus appeared again, but in a different way this time. He looked at me with a loving smile, almost human. He welcomed me in His arms with such affection and tenderness, something I've never experienced before in the arms of a man.

Of a man?!

What am I saying here?

Yes, it's true, I felt that Jesus was now offering me the love of a man. The human love and the Divine love were merged in Him.

I did it!

Yes, I was able to merge and live the two types of love instantly, in a pure and absolute way.

God, can it be real what I am feeling?

I felt I was in love with Jesus, and He, in return, was offering me the love of a Lover.

This was so new and unexpected that I didn't know how to react. I had never seen myself like this before, as His lover. My mind was still blocked, contemplating the idea of desecration...

This is not possible; my mind would have said before. But I was so in love and the love I felt from Him was so beautiful and big and complete that I could not resist it.

More than that, any embarrassment or guilt disappeared.

The karmic burden related to earthly love was instantly burnt.

This was a really interesting experience. I saw how all the hopes, attachments, frustrations and many other states related to loving a man had all gone.

It was a Divine gift.

Detachment and pure love replaced all the expectations, frustrations and wounds from my soul.

I felt how years or maybe lifetimesof karma can be burnt in an instant. I felt both His love and my love for Him inside me, a love that had maybe appeared in this form in another life, which now I was able to remember.

I felt He **is** my Lover, the One I'd been waiting for all my life.

Here I was, in love with Jesus.

I felt I was His lover.

The feeling was complete on all levels of my being. My chest was vibrating with love, my heart was racing, happiness surrounded me, I felt I was awakened as a woman by His masculinity. My erotic energies awakened and were instantly sublimated into my heart chakra and in the Sahasrara, the crown chakra. I was simultaneously experiencing orgasm, love and bliss.

Now I understood the line from the Christening - *And I will unite myself with Christ* - and also the notion of **Divine Eros** mentioned in certain books.

This state lasted for months, and not just for a moment.

I received the Divine gift after pain, prayers and despair.

I understood then that the one who left me with a broken heart was just an instrument, playing his role in my life.

If he hadn't left, I would have never known Divine Love.

I was blessed with the surprising state of feeling Jesus both as a Lord and as a Lover. Is it this state that the nuns want to attain when they wish to become the Brides of Christ? Who knows? Maybe it is.

My first tendency was towards celibacy, again. I thought Jesus was expecting this sacrifice from me. But His answer came quickly: He was not asking me that. On the contrary, if my soul desired, I could have all the lovers I wanted.

I was not as I was before. Once I received His love, I could direct it towards any man I wanted. Jesus knew that, but I didn't. My mind was not ready to understand the transformation that took place in my consciousness.

I was an adult but was thinking like a child. It took me a while to understand all that happened then and how my life would unfold from that moment on.

Jesus allowed me to have lovers. Hmmm. He was not jealous. It sounded very funny to me.

But can a man who truly loves be jealous?

He is more than just a man.

When He said -*If you love your father or mother or brothers more than you love Me, you are not loving me at all* -He was not saying that out of jealousy.

He is no egoist to want all the love just for Himself.

By giving ourselves completely to Him we have the chance to receive all His love, a love that comprises everything.

I understood this later in life and I will explain it later in the book, respecting the sequence of events. When you receive information all at once, your mind freezes, it cannot work anymore. But it needs time to understand.

Now I was seeing God in Love!

Yes, it's true, God is in love with His Creation. This is a great Truth.

And if He is offering us all we wish for with all His love... why wouldn't He offer us the love of a Lover? Is there a problem there, a restriction? He can't, He doesn't want to? That's not true. He can, He wants to and He is not jealous.

Many girls are waiting and dreaming of an Ideal Lover.

He is the Ideal Lover. God is the Ideal Lover.

I recognised in Jesus all the qualities of the Perfect Lover.

He was very careful with me from all points of view, the way an ideal lover, partner, husband should be. He was always with me and never, not even once, did I feel I was left alone. Any woman who is in love wishes that her loved one is with her every moment. He was offering me His love constantly. Waves and waves of love were poured onto me. Sometimes all that love made breathing difficult for me, almost suffocating me. For the physical body, it is always difficult to receive all that God has to offer.

His gifts were both physical and subtle. He was offering me spiritual gifts, He was exemplifying states, He was teaching me many things. He helped me understand many life situations, He was answering my questions and, at the same time, He was awakening me as a woman and fulfilling me. No, I didn't have fantasies about making love to Jesus. My physical body was awakened, polarised by Jesus, the man, but lovemaking was not necessary to 'calm' those energies. Jesus took care of my energies and transformed them into cosmic orgasms. He was doing everything. I was assisting, witnessing the transformations that took place in my body, my mind, my soul and my spirit. Or maybe I was not a witness but more like the main guest at a feast.

My menstruation started to sublimate also.

What does sublimation mean and how do I see that?

Let's remember the monks who adopt abstinence. The creative energy that we lose through our menstruation (for women) or ejaculation (for men) is actually a loss of the divine creative potential given to our beings. This loss creates a distance between us and God. There are spiritual societies, family centred, where the husband and wife make love only when they wish to procreate. They don't want to lose the divine creative potential that they've been endowed with.

Other societies make love without the discharging of sexual fluids, practicing so called sexual continence. Again, they aim for the same purpose.

That creative potential can be used and there's no need to throw it out of the body. Being a divine creative potential, it means it is a creative energy we dispose of and we can use it in our creations and daily life. We can direct this energy to every part of our being and we can use it as we please. It is like an infinite energy at our disposal.

How can you explain the exhaustion, the tiredness, the decrease of our levels of awarenessand consciousness? And many times, the fights that appear after and later, the divorces?

Why lose when we can win?

It's like having an immense energy and instead of using it, we throw it away. What for? For a second of pleasure, of illusion. But if we can control these energies and if we know how to use them, the pleasure is even greater and there are other benefits too.

Jesus exemplified in me this process of sublimation of the creative energy. I was seeing this transformation occurring in my body and, at the same time, I was enjoying all the pleasure and satisfaction that appeared on all levels of my being.

We need to remember that the human being has seven chakras, or wheels of energy, and sexual pleasure is related to the second chakra, Swadhistana. But you can experience very complex and beautiful states on each of the other chakras. There are worlds and universes unknown to some. You can read about them, but discovering them and experiencing them yourself is totally different.

Under the protection and direct guidance of Jesus, I enjoyed these complete states for months. Since that point, my path was ascending. All these experiences opened my mind and my soul.

I knew that the people who are in love are very happy. And so was I. I was very happy and in love.

Yes, it was true, Jesus was not jealous, but he was offering me such fulfilment that I felt no need to be in a relationship with another man. He was giving me everything so I started my period of abstinence. All my energy, my mind, my feelings were related to Him.

I was constantly thinking about Him, living with Him; I was connected to Him.

Living like this for a long period of time, I noticed the advantages of having Jesus (or God) as our Lover. Here are some of them:

1. **A permanent state of happiness** – Being God's lover, you permanently feel waves of love flowing from your heart. They always activate your Anahata Chakra and they reverberate in all your being. This state of love, without an object – the only object that can be is God – gives you a state

of permanent happiness. After a while, love is associated with happiness and you will say: *I feel happiness flowing from me*. Sometimes, when I felt that, I would say: *I am so happy!* and those around me, not seeing an external reason for my happiness, would ask me: *And why are you happy now?* I would answer: *Well, I don't know…just like that… for no reason… I just am!*

You are like a lunatic, singing and dancing everywhere, at home, on the street, hugging everyone, loving, falling in love with everything, laughing. Those who see Him can't understand Him because His external appearance is misleading (He is in rags, He has nothing to eat). But does that matter?! All the joy and happiness in the world dwells in His heart. What else would matter?!

2. **A permanent state of fulfilment** – Having your heart full of love, this happiness also generates a state of fulfilment on every level. You feel you have everything, that nothing is lacking. It is said that *All is Love*, that *God is Love*. And when you feel loved, you need nothing else. And when you are not loved, no matter how much you have, it's as though you have nothing… Every person feels the need to love and be loved by someone – a dog, a cat, any living being. But when you feel the immense love that God pours on you, an unparalleled state of plenitude appears in your soul.

3. **A state of erotic plenitude** –Just like they describe it in the story of Krishna and his *gopis*, God makes love to you. You experience erotic feelings, cosmic orgasms on different chakras, especially at the level of the Anahata Chakra and you end up not feeling the need for a man (or woman) in the physical world. I was always in a state of orgasm. My whole body was crossed by shivers of pleasure. Every second felt like I was making love with the most extraordinary man in the world. The pleasure was not just erotic. It started there and it transformed into **Divine Eros**, that state where love and eroticism melt into devotion.

4. **A state of perfect health** –When happiness is permanently flowing through your body, you cannot be sick! What is

sickness? It is energy blocked on a certain level. When is it that the energy stops flowing properly? When our mind is constantly 'chewing' on small nothings that bother us. When you are happy, the process is inverted: the happiness frees our mind and thus the energy will flow freely and in harmony through our being. In this way, all the mental and physical blockages are eliminated and we become healthy or we don't get sick anymore.

It is still possible for some illnesses to appear, either because of an accelerated karmic burning or simply because you have madesome mistakes that need to be repaid. That is the case when we are not liberated beings. But these sicknesses are healed rapidly and even paranormal healings can occur. The access to divine healing energies is easier. In these moments, your prayers for being healed are going straight to the source. Your prayers have power. I'll always remember this comparison that someone made in a conference: *It is not the same if an ant addresses an elephant or if a lion does it.* When you are small (in faith) your voice can barely be heard, but as you grow, it becomes stronger.

Let me give you an example: I was volunteering in a city three hours away from home. For fifteen years, everything was good and I was happy to be able to help. But after a while, my soul was not fulfilled. The mission I had received from God was on hold, time was passing and I felt I couldn't postpone it anymore. In my mind, I thought that I needed to stop this voluntary work and take care of the mission that was assigned by God. I spoke to the organisers, to the leaders, but they didn't understand me and my program remained the same. I was not getting any free days, nobody was trying to find a solution that would help me... It was like a broken mechanism that was operating without regard for people's souls. Nobody asked if you could come or not, you had to be there. My subconscious mind caught the idea that I don't want to go there and it started to find ways to stop me from going there.

So, every evening before I had to go there, I would get sick. Today a cold, the next time another small problem, and so on for a year – a year of continuously asking the leaders, unsuccessfully, to understand that I can't go anymore – till I got sciatica. Till then, I kept going there even though I was sick, but the sciatica crisis gave me such great pain in my leg that sometimes I could not walk. Although I was in a crisis, I would go if I was able to walk, but on two occasions I ended up needing help. I would go there alone, believing that the pain would disappear on the way there, but it was not the case. It was not only my subconscious, but it was also God who wanted me to stop going there. But I was so responsible and correct in my actions that I needed their approval first.

The first time when I left home in a crisis, I needed someone's help on my way back - to get me to the railway station and put me on the train. The second time, after a night of excruciating pain, again, someone had to get me to a bus to go home and once I arrived at my destination, another person had to help me disembark from the bus. At that point, I said enough was enough. I decided to do something to get rid of the sciatica. It was not a punishment from God. I simply needed to stop my volunteering activities and continue with something else. So there was no reason why I would not receive the healing grace. My soul was sincere, I wanted to help, but I couldn't anymore. There was no hidden agenda.

I started to pray for healing. After three days, the next phenomenon occurred: I felt how the point on my spine, where the nerve root is, started to vibrate and to heat up until I felt it burning. The burning came down the spine to my coccyx and it continued to burn for half an hour. After that, I was completely healed. Before that, I was in such a state that I couldn't bend or flex my spine in any direction. After half an hour, I was able to move as I wished and the problems have never returned. My spine is now as flexible as it was when I was fifteen years old.

But my volunteering work continued because the organisers didn't understand my reasons. Then God intervened and got me out of there. Something shocking came up for me, not allowing the progress of the cause (continuing to go there). The leaders of the organisation accused me of wanting to steal something and removed me. It was on flimsy grounds. What they said was that I had tried to steal an initiationthat I had already received from them a few years before. It was so absurd! But if they were not willing to understand in the beginning, God found a method to stop me going there as only He understood the situation.

After fifteen years I left the place ashamed, losing this time not to a person I loved, but to the community I had lived in for over twenty-five years. All my friends, all my life was there.

I didn't have the time to cry and victimise myself because in three months' time I was already in India with a visa and a contract with a university where I went to teach the Romanian language.

God works in mysterious ways!

If that was not God's wish, how would I have got to the university in India when I was not even fluent in English?!

Those who want to go and teach at a university abroad have to pass difficult exams. There is a lot of effort put into getting such a position. But for me, everything went smoothly.

When I was interviewed for the position in Romania, at the university that sent me to India, the Dean told me when she saw me: *I know you, I trust you, I've seen your lectures about the Angels.* That was the extent of my interview. I then received the papers for going to India.

India welcomed me with a lot of love. Everybody - teachers and students - restored my confidence and healed my soul. And India, through what it is, awakened my spirit. I met a professor there who arranged a tour for me and my theatre when he found out I had a theatre group.

Since then, we had several tours with the theatre and all were a great success.

New friendships were created, new relationships and collaborations arose, changing my life.

It was then, during that trip, that the idea for writing this book came up, once my soul found its peace and reconciled.

I have narrated this story in brief, so you would understand that nothing is by chance. Not even a sickness, when we truly give ourselves to the Divine. He takes care of us from all points of view. Everything is part of a Divine Plan.

Remember this: God has no intention of harming us.

Remember Him in times of sickness, ask Him to heal you and He will grant it for sure.

Let me give you one more example.

Sometimes I would get a powerful headache, localised on a point on the left side on the back of my head. From there the pain would spread through my entire head with such intensity that I would feel my head was about to explode. I would cry from the intensity of the pain. Unfortunately, it started to repeat itself quiteoften and I began to worry that it might be something serious. I would feel very weak duringthose moments.

One evening, during one such moment, before going to bed, I asked the Angels of Health to cure me. Because the pain was not going away, I thought about asking Jesus for help and I uttered the following:

My Lord, my adored Beloved, please send me your Light Angels to heal me.

His answer came instantly:

Alright, but you know that my intention would be enough for you to heal.

I immediately felt a vibrating point that was a bit above and more to the right than the one I knew and gradually, the pain disappeared.

After a short time, it was gone, completely and forever.

Thank you, Lord!

This is how you healed many of my sicknesses.

Once my confidence increased, I started using the prayers for any health problem that appeared, even for a broken finger that occurred later on.

5. **Reversing the aging process or slowing it** - What is it that makes us grow old? Worries, fears, sorrows, efforts, disappointments, shortages, etc.

   All these disappear when we are embraced by God. Once we give ourselves to Him, He will give us everything in return.

6. **We donot feel loneliness anymore** – God is always with us, close to us. Day and night, His presence can be felt. This is as real as it can be. He is always embracing us. We will never feel lonely anymore, even if we are alone on the peak of a mountain.

   While on the subject, you need to know that loneliness is also an advantage in your relationship with God. If you are not alone in the room, your attention gets distracted. Solitude and isolation are recommended for communicating with the Angels, with Jesus or with God.

   Even if you are married, chose to sleep in separate rooms because God is speaking to you in those intimate moments, communicating with your soul. Late in the night, when I was alone, I would often hear angelic choirs. It is a sublime experience to hear them: the music is divine and the state that they create is very special... I once heard a choir singing hymns of glory! Loving Him so much, I felt at some moments that the only way I could express my gratitude was by singing hymns of praise to Him. What else canyou do but praise Him when He is everything and He offers you all you need with infinite love? What else canyou do but praise Him when you are floating in an ocean of Divine Love?!

7. **We are never again frustrated** – There is no reason why we would be... He is fulfilling us on every level.

8. **We don't get upset** – If sometimes you feel upset, it is because we are vulnerable and we live in a world that is

not all that perfect. But, He will come as a playful lover, taking you in His arms and saying: *Let it be, my dear, these things shouldn't bother you...* and in the next minute He takes away your sadness and melts it in His love.

9. **We are no longer envious** –There is no need to be. We are the ones loved by God and we have all we need.

10. **We are no longer jealous** – For a while you might think that you are the only one to receive such a love and that for some miraculous reason you deserve it. Yes, it's true, you deserve it, but the more you deepen in this Divine Love, the more you will realise that it is for everyone. And when all is given to you, you won't feel the love as being divided when it is given to someone else too. And the same is also valid for material goods. No matter how much you would give from the Divine Whole, it will still be a whole because you too are a part of this whole. It is never divided. You will be one with the Whole and you will never feel any shortage. Can you then speak about jealousy anymore?

11. **The relationship with our partner (lover, husband, wife, etc.) becomes more harmonious** – This is because all expectations disappear. When expectations are there, the relationship stops working: I want you to be like this, I want you to do this and that and so on… We have all been through it! But when God gives us everything and we are completely fulfilled, what else can we ask from someone? We are not expecting anything because we don't lack anything. And so, magically, the relationship becomes free. At last, we are free! We are then able to love each other and to simply understand each other.

12. **A feeling of reliability appears in this life and also beyond it, in the ones to come** – Once God has declared His love for us, there is no turning back. He won't change His mind. A sense of reliability appears. We have His love for eternity. You feel it with you now and forever, in all the lives to come and in between them, in all the worlds and forever.

13. **A constant state of sublimation** – It's amazing how He sublimates your inferior feelings. He simply won't let

you hold onto them for more than five or seven minutes. He instantly takes you up, in His love. And He does that without you having to ask for it, without practicing any sublimation techniques. Once in His arms, He takes care of you in all aspects.

14. **You will get the job according to your mission** - If your job is exhausting you, if you don't like it, if it annoys you, this means it is not respecting your mission. You are not yet integrated into the Divine Harmony. In other words, you are still quite far away from Deification. The closer you get to God, the easier it is to communicate with Him directly. Once you achieve a real communion with Him (and not an imaginary one), you will get closer to achieving your purpose in life.

    You may say that not all jobs are enjoyable. But yes, all of them are beautiful and there are people born for each job. For some, hammering nails can be a real pleasure, for others the pleasure might come from cleaning or taking care of the sick, etc.

    We find a job unpleasant when our place is not there.

    By getting closer to God, we also get closer to our place in this Universe until we reach the place that was destined for us. It is not a problem if we change jobs. And it is not a flaw if we didn't spend years with every company where we were employed. As we evolve, our activities will match the level of our consciousness. When we arrive at the right place, we might stay there for the rest of our lives, even if it's hard work. It will bring us joy and happiness, it will fulfil our soul. The fear ofwhat might happen tomorrow is a big worry. Sometimes it feels like we need to make an effort to stay at the same workplace for all our lives (especially if we are earning a good salary), but we must always remember that everything is in God's hands and not in ours.

    Let's receive His love and allow Him to make us Happy!

GIFTS

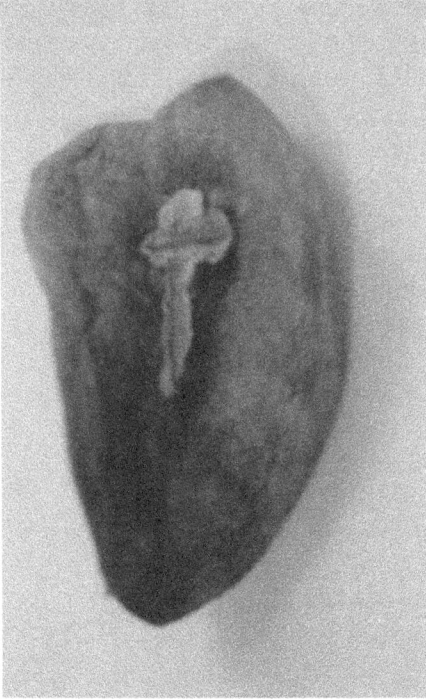

I would often receive gifts from Jesus.
Once He materialised as a cross on a potato slice. I was slicing potatoes for the meal I was preparing. During one of my states of deep communion with Him, a cross appeared inside the potato I was preparing. I placed the slice aside and after a while, as it began to dry, the cross became more visible. I was shaken by its sight. You could feel Jesus' touch on it.

Another gift appeared once on my birthday. It was a state. I had the vision of a martyrdom. The Christian martyr in my vision was burned at the stake. Against all human expectations, he didn't suffer at all. When the fire was lit, Jesus bestowed His Grace upon him, making him experience a state of communion with the Divine Eros. In other words, he was in ecstasy, in complete communion with God, feeling His love in all his being. In that ecstatic state, all the pain disappeared. He left this world in ecstasy, without suffering. Through empathy, I was able to feel a glimpse of his state. What I understood then was that when you die, if you offer yourself completely to Jesus or to God, He takes you in His arms immediately and protects you from suffering.

We need to remember all the martyr saints that were put on a stake and didn't burn, like Saint Emilian. He was thrown into a fire and not only did he not suffer, but his body was not touched by the flames.

The vision was a special gift, both a surprise and an important lesson – God will protect you from all suffering when you are truly devoted to Him.

The notion that once you are on a path towards God you need to suffer is a false one. And false also are the ones stating that upon hearing His call, you will be tested or that you need to struggle in order to reach God.

Why would people ever want to reach God if they associate Him with struggles, sufferance, penitence, fasting and lack?

On the contrary, once on the path, God takes away your suffering.

Lately I've heard some modernist ideas, like the one that you can't reach God if you live in luxury and comfort. These wrong ideas do nothing more than distance people from the real God. If God is plenitude, love, beauty, harmony and all that is wonderful in the world, how could it be possible that we, who are made in His resemblance, would have to choose sufferance, lack, poverty, struggle, etc, in order to reach Him, to be with Him?

Someone once said that you cannot think you will go straight into His Kingdom upon death if you haven't found Him here first. When you understand how the Law of Resonance works, you realise the truth in this affirmation.

If you look for God everywhere, you will be surprised to find plenitude, happiness and satisfaction in everything.

He is everywhere, all is Complete.

When you quit beauty, fulfilment or love, you are quitting God.

Another one of His impressive gifts was…a garden of pines. Yes, you are hearing the truth. I love pines and I always wanted to have a pine tree in my garden, either the one from home or that from the guesthouse. For a few years in a row, I would bring small pine trees from the forest and I would plant them in pots or in the garden, but none of them survived. I felt very sad that I couldn't decorate my garden with pines. One of those years, in the spring time, around twenty small pine trees appeared beyond the fence of the guesthouse, on land that also belonged to us. They were really small (two hands length) and they had just appeared there. It was like someone had planted them, but it was not anyone from the family. That land was a pasture and they wanted to keep it clean because it enabled them to receive EU grants.

You can imagine my surprise and the thrill I felt when I saw so many pine trees in my garden! I walked through them with so much joy!

Year after year, I protected them from my family - who wanted to keep the pasture clean - until they grew to be about a metre high.

Every time I look at them now, a feeling of joy and gratitude fills my heart, knowing that they are a gift from God.

SHIVA

At ayoga course I was attending, we were learning about Hinduism. We were initiated in different divine aspects belonging to the Hindu culture. That was very useful for me. This way I learned about India, which in my opinion is the cradle of spirituality on this planet. This knowledge opened the door to a whole new world for me, allowing me to step towards the Orient where I discovered a very fulfilling culture.

I had already visited India a number of times. At the yoga course, we had been initiated into communion with Shiva, Shakti, Kali, Tara and other Hindu deities.

Each place holds the traces of certain feelings and beliefs.

I was learning about these Hindu deities, I was believing in them, but I never really felt them till I arrived in India. There, as soon as you entered a temple dedicated to Shiva, you willfeel His presence. Or in a temple dedicated to Vishnu, you willfeel Vishnu. I experienced the same feeling in the temples of Krishna, Durga, Parvati, etc. My yoga practice, my prayers and my meditations had all prepared my physical body so that the trips to India were fascinating through the specific feelings for each of the temples. It seemed amazing, but it was really like meeting that deity there.

But my attachment to Jesus was not allowing me to completely welcome Shiva into my heart.

A new lesson was offered to me.

And that was an important chapter in my life.

One evening in Romania, I attended a ritual where an aspect of Shiva was worshipped. It was the aspect of Chandrashekara, the one who wears the moon. It was beautiful. It lasted for a couple of hours and then, later in the night, I went home troubled. I was asking myself: *But God, why don't they also perform rituals to worship Jesus?* In my opinion Jesus was everything, and it seemed normal that such celebrations would also be consecrated to Him. That question and the frustration I was feeling affected my sleep. I writhed in bed for a while and then my good and dear Jesus answered me:

…is an aspect of God…

Because of my ignorance and stupidity, Jesus had to answer me Himself that it was worshipped as an aspect of God.

Every time Jesus or God tell you something, it's like an initiation, an induction. That Truth penetrates your spirit and you feel it in all your being. From that moment on, that Truth lives in you.

Understanding that Divine aspects were adored through these celebrations reassured me. It was alright. No Divine principle was being violated.

Those images of the Cosmic Powers - of Shakti, of Shiva, of Vishnu, etc - were actually Divine aspects and there was nothing wrong in worshipping them. Through the action of worshipping, you were just bringing them closer to you. Whenever you need to develop a quality, an aspect of your life or you need help on a certain level, you can achieve it by devoting yourself to one of His aspects, instead of directly asking Him. The moment you understand the Hindu symbols, you can understand their faith.

God can sometimes appear too abstract and distant for humans. That's why, on different paths, intelligent people translated the faith into the human language. So, in Hinduism you will find Brahma – the Creator, Vishnu – the Preserver, Shiva – the Destroyer, Kali – the energy of time, Tara – the energy of compassion, Tripura Sundari – the energy of beauty, and so on.

Through meditations, Buddha understood the most abstract aspects of creation and divinity. He asked his disciples to eliminate all their desires, thoughts and attachments and to preserve a pure mind, just likecrystal. But the way he said it was too abstract for the following generations of Buddhists. So they needed to speak in a way everyone would understand. They gave names to energies, states, sentiments and forms of consciousness and they also assigned a divinity to each.

That was how the Dhyani-Buddha, the Heruka and other Buddhist deities appeared.

By studying each religion or path towards God you are able to find their logic, although hidden under many 'helpers' and steps

Jesus used stories and parables to transmit His teachings.

I invite everyone to be understanding, to study a bit, to have an open mind and heart, before saying that he is on the right path to God, that his path is the best one, the most efficient one, the real one.

The more you say you are on the right path, the further you go from the Truth.

I am telling you this now because I did the same and the Divine answer appeared without delay.

In my mind, there was still the greatest separation. Jesus was Jesus, God was God, Shiva was Shiva. I didn't know where to find Them all and how to get Them all together.

Which is the Greatest? Which of them is really God? To whom should I pray?

Those questions tormented me for a while until, one day, the Divine answer came:

Shiva, Jesus and God are One.

This time the answer came from the Virgin Mary. I had an image of the Virgin Mary on the wall and my soul was crying to the sky. I needed an answer. I tried to meditate and I ended my meditation shouting out this question. I couldn't find peace.

My eyes remained on Her image and the answer came from Her.

HELPERS

We believe ourselves to be separated, isolated and abandoned.

Someone once said with disappointment:

God doesn't listen to my prayers.

He was praying for a certain type of motorcycle and his wish wasn't granted immediately. After two years, he owned the best motorcycle in the country.

It's wrong to believe that God is not listening to us. He and also Jesus, the Angels, the Virgin Mary, the Saints and the Enlightened Masters are all listening to us and helping us. Sometimes the answer to our prayers have not yet been addressed.

I was shouting to the sky and my hope was that someone would answer. And it happened.

Once, a person close to my heart suffered an injustice. His words were recorded and then twisted, taken out of context and used against him. He was publicly reproved and punished. Knowing he was not guilty (but there must have been a karmic necessity for it to happen), he was very sad. He had beenbetrayed by one of his good friends. It was as though the universe had collapsed on him. Someone took a picture of him during that time and the contrast was huge. You could have titled the picture – a sad man in paradise.

Whenever injustice happens, God cannot step on the free will of the ones who do wrong. He will compensate the oppressed one though by offering him His Grace.

My friend was in a very special place, the Bay of Kotor, a paradise on earth. The sunset there was sublime. He was sittingon the terrace of a house with a sea view. The house had its own private beach and there was no conditioning except the burden on his soul. It seemed as ifthe pain he was feeling couldn't be erased. He was betrayed by a good friend, in a community where you were judged and punished without getting the chance to defend yourself. Are there still places like that in the twenty-first century? Yes, there are in the places where people believe they are greater than God.

He was on vacation. He had visited Medjugorje and, on his way to Greece, he had stopped in the Bay of Kotor.

By chance, he also visited the island of Evia, where you can find the relics of Saint John the Russian. He didn't plan to go there, and he did not know of the place or of the Saint. It was clear that he was guided there by the Divine. In front of the relics, the miracle happened. His soul was cured and the situation was left aside. The karma had been burnt. A Divine hand took away his burden and even more, the Divine Justice manifested itself. Whenever a pure-hearted, good-intentioned man is harmed, the Divine Justice will be manifested rapidly. He returned home with a healed soul, light as a feather. In a few months, he had the chance to go on a spiritual tour acrossIndia. It was another Divine gift. During his trip, he received the news of the death of his friend, the one who had betrayed him. He was thevictim of a terrible car accident.

I never wished him any harm – hekept repeating this to himself whenhe heard the news. And that was true. Since his visit to the relics of Saint John the Russian, his soul had been healed and was full of forgiveness.

I mention this story so that you can see that sometimes, the answers and the help come from those we least expect. We just need to believe and abandon ourselves. We are not alone. There are many watching over us and helping us.

I'll tell you another story:

I hadjust been introduced to this person and I knew little about him.

It happened duringthe period when I had started to see Jesus as Light. I was sharing the same room with that person and we were resting in bed. Shortly after I fell asleep, through astral projection, I left my body and I saw the room with all that there was in it, including our bodies resting on the bed.

Next to the bed, I saw the Virgin Mary kneeling and praying for that person. She was dressed in black, gazing atthe sky and tears were pouringout of her eyes. With all her being, she was praying to Jesus and her prayers were immediately reaching God. I could see that.

I witnessed this spiritual scene with great amazement. The Virgin Mary was here, in this small room, on her knees, humbly praying? Why? Was there something bad about to happen? What was I to believe out of this?

Why had I seen this?

As I told you, I never had a religious education and I never prayed to the Virgin Mary. I respected her because she gave birth to Jesus, but I never thought of reaching out to her. There was no reason why this vision of her would appear to me.

That taught me a lot about praying and fidelity.

I was 'seeing' Virgin Mary's prayer going up to Jesus and also its intensity, her faith and her unconditional love.

I immediately told the other person about my vision and he was surprised, amazed and also slightly indifferent about the Virgin Mary. Years have passed since that incident.

That person had other belief; he was devoted to Lord Shiva, so he neglected what I told him. But I couldn't forget that episode.

Over time, there were very tense and critical moments when it seemed as if there was no visible way out of escape for that person. Then, I would pray to the Virgin Mary to help him and - you have to believe me - the help came instantly. Each time, it was a miracle. The only explanation was that in another life, he must have offered his being to the Virgin Mary and now, for the rest of his existence, the Mother of Christ was faithful to him.

Have I made myself clear? The person I'm talking about does believe in the Virgin Mary, but that's all. He had never prayed to her in this life, except for when he was experiencing some very difficult times. In this life,he did nothing to create this connection, no effort was put into receiving her love.

But from the outside, as a witness, I can see all the love and help that this person receives from the Virgin Mary.

Often, we are unaware of who is loving us and how great that love is.

They are always with us, they don't forget about us, they don't abandon us even when we forget about them.

I thank them with all my soul.

GOD IS ONE

Returning to the answer I received, the three notions - Jesus, Shiva and God - reunited in my consciousness and my heart. Once and for all I understood that they are One and this understanding extended to all notions about God that exist or have existed. The God that people went into battles for is One and the same, just known under different names.

With this I began a new phase in my life when I found God everywhere.

I meditated in all types of churches, in prayer houses, in ruins, in mosques, in temples, in pyramids and, guess what, God was in each of them.

I visited many sacred places on this planet and, while the tourists were taking pictures and filming, I would search for a quiet place to meditate in. Was I searching for God? No, I didn't have to search for Him in places anymore. My pleasure was in discovering how He is loved, how He is worshipped by the devotees of that religion, of that spiritual path.

This is how I started my spiritual travels. I would visit places - not to see them and take pictures of them - but to feel how the people there (and also their ancestors) expressed their faith.

I remember an experience I had in the Garden of Gethsemane.

I was walking through that sacred place with adoration and reverence. It is said that the olive trees have been there since the time of Jesus. I meditated in different places where it is said that Jesus walked and also in front of the church where the stone on which Jesus prayed is placed.

At some point, I clearly felt His presence. My mind immediately thought that maybe I had lived in the times of Jesus but His answer came quickly:

You were not with me then, I am with you now!

You cannot imagine how grateful I was! To feel Him and hear Him there, in that sacred place... Thanks to His Will and His Grace that I was able to feel Him and to receive His answer.

This way, every place I visited was becoming a spiritual experience for me.

This explains why I still travel to India, fascinated by its spirituality, although I am in love with Jesus and it is through Him that I reached God.

I posted articles and images from my trips in India on Facebook. A Muslim friend of mine, seeing me in the middle of the statues, asked me (with the best of intentions) what I was doing there and what I hoped to find because (according to him) God certainly isn't in those stones. Yes, the Muslim faith doesn't accept depicting Allah through images or in statues. But God is everywhere, in every form, in love, in Eros, in the landscapes and so on. By meditating there, in the middle of those statues, I was feeling how the devotees of that path felt God.

I was delighted with how God is felt and loved in the Blue Mosque in Istanbul or in other mosques in India and also in several other places I visited.

I loved the feeling I had while meditating in the Egyptian pyramids.

You have a certain way of feeling God. Each one of us feels Him differently. It is delightful to be able to feel what others are feeling forHim. Instead of watching TV, show after show, in complete monotony, for me it is of far greater pleasure to close my eyes and feel God in different cultures and places.

THRESHOLD

In the same way, I received answers for my questions, I could also see many other things far more clearly. I was meditating with Jesus for hours. He was my only focus. I just wanted to be with Him.

During one meditation, I felt intense love in my heart. It expanded and all the world was love. The love in my heart and the love in the Universe became One inside me. All was an ocean of love. I was melting in that love.

Back then, I had already experienced moments when I would go beyond the threshold. That's how I named it - threshold. Actually, it's like a gate that takes you to a different level of consciousness. Initially it was just for a few minutes, then for a few hours and then days. I was experiencing a state of fulfilment, a feeling that I have everything. There was no feeling of lack or unfulfillment. All the world seemed to be mine and I was living in a paradise of plenitude. Along with the love in my heart and that which was surrounding me, an unconditional love, there was also a state of continuous happiness without any obvious reason. I was just experiencing constant and continuous happiness.

When I returned from the threshold, I once again experienced the state of lacking. I couldn't understand what was taking me beyond the threshold and what kept bringing me back.

I just noticed the different states and a desire to permanently exist beyond the threshold.

The period of Grace continued, Jesus was always with me, watching over me and helping me in all of life's situations.

I became used to receiving what I needed and also experiencing the love that Jesus was giving me.

Sometimes, I went beyond the threshold to a totally different state but I was always returned to this world of illusions and attachments.

I remember that an expansion of my aura followed the entrance into that realm.

Life went on naturally, with everything, that is.

Once I met a man whose masculine qualities were so evident and I admired that about him. There were no other thoughts or desires. I just noticed him. I was still in love with Jesus and very happy with His company.

A test followed.

When I was home alone, I had a clear feeling of a demon approaching me and whispering in my ear: *If you can have all that you want, why don't you ask to be loved by...* (and he whispered this man's name).

My answer came rapidly, with no hesitation: *Jesus is my lover and never in this world will I want another one!*

I rejected the idea of replacing Jesus with an earthly lover with all my might.

Then, all of a sudden, something happened: I felt Jesus in front of me, emanating Love and Light. He approached me and embraced me. Our hearts united and I melted in His being. I was gone. It was just one heart, ours, vibrating and growing, expanding across the world. I felt I was in the centre of the world and from there, from the heart, the Universe was created and started its expansion.

From that point on, wherever I was physically, my heart was in the centre of the world, of the universe and expanded itself.

It was not my heart, but the one that remained One, after the union of my heart with the heart of Jesus.

My heart remained united with His heart and as I think about this, I can feel, even now, how Jesus expands the universe in His heart.

That was the moment when I stepped over the threshold for eternity.

From that moment, every feeling of lacking completely disappeared from my life. I felt I have it all; I experienced a continuous state of happiness and fulfilment.

From that point on, God, love, happiness and plenitude were always with me. Everything was there. I was experiencing that state with or without a physical manifestation.

I stepped onto a new level of my life.

You might ask me: *You really had everything? You were never upset anymore? No other difficulties appeared in your life?*

The story doesn't end there.

For a few months, I experienced that bliss. I was exploding with happiness and love. I laughed all the time and all my life was a dance.

Part II

GOD'S LOVE

I AM THE WAY

This plenitude, this joy and happiness, this ecstasy in the heart of Jesus lasted for a couple of months. Until one day, Jesus disappeared. I clearly remember the exact place and moment where that happened.

But not for a second did I feel abandoned. God took the place of Jesus.

Is there any difference between them?

The Father and I are One – said Jesus. But He is also saying that the Father is The Father and nobody, not even Jesus, can comprise Him.

I experienced the Truth uttered by Jesus – ***I am the Path, the Truth and Life.***

Yes, He was my path to God.

Jesus guided me to God, as I've described in this book.

With infinite patience and understanding, with love and kindness, He guided me step by step till I was in the arms of God.

Until that moment, I was happily in love with Jesus.From that point on I was a thousand times happier and more in love with God.

The moment Jesus was gone, I instantly felt God taking His place.

He entered me and I felt my relationship with Him. I felt I loved Him beyond any love before and simultaneously, I felt loved as I'd never been loved in my life.

I became obsessed with God. My mind was with Him in every moment. I couldn't bear being apart from Him, not even for a second, a second when my thought would be directed to Jesus or another deity. God was present in my mind, in my soul, in my breath. God was my life. He was always on my mind. I was in love with Him to the paramount state of being in love. I was obsessed with Him. I was crazy about Him.

I desperately loved Him, I loved all of Him. All of a sudden, my life became God. Nothing else in this world interested me.

God took Jesus' place in my heart, I was in love with Him and He became my lover.

That state of not being separated from my beloved Lover, God, lasted for eight months. Throughout this time, I was burning with desire and love for Him. He was permanently with me. The more I felt Him, the more I yearned for Him. My thirst for Him reached unimaginable heights.

He was so real and alive in my life that I wanted to pick up the phone and call Him.

I would close myself in the room. I had periods of isolation because, as an egotistic lover, I felt He was there and I didn't want to ever let Him leave.

My friends were participating in other spiritual activities and doing other meditations but for me, God was the air I was breathing. He was my life.

Sometimes I would cry in despair. I was crying because I was longing for Him.

Don't ever think I am saying that He abandoned me for an instant or that for a second I didn't feel Him. That was the paradox. The more I felt Him, the more I would call for Him.

Sometimes I was afraid He might disappear, He might leave me. I couldn't bear the idea of never again being able to feel Him. With tears pouring from my eyes, I would pray to Him to always be with me, to never leave me. I was praying He would keep the eyes of my soul open so that I could see Him both awake and in my sleep, no matter whether my physical eyes were open or closed.

Only once in my life had I ever experienced a similar state before this period of grace. I've felt God before, but never with such intensity.

I was in India.

This is precisely why I love this country so much, because of all the exceptional experiences I've had there.

I was visiting Arunachala, the mountain where Shiva manifested as a Linga of Fire and where Sri Ramana Maharshi attained liberation. As I climbed the mountain, I had a great burden on my back that increased the effort. We were barefoot. As the mountain is holy, we had to leave our shoes at the base. First, we visited the two caves of Maharshi and we meditated there. Then we climbed to the top of the mountain. We sat on the hot rock and relaxed; we contemplated everything and we meditated. We had the whole city at our feet and also the Fire Temple. What a splendid view it was!

Gradually we went beyond the realm of time. We were suspended in another reality.

We stayed there for as long as we felt the need. We were completely free, both on the outside and the inside. Nobody had put a limit to our stay there and our souls were free of tension.

As we started our descent, I was amazed to realise that I felt very relieved. It seemed as if I was floating. It wasn't because we had put in great effort to climb up the mountain and now the descent was easier. It was something else. Up there, we were immersed in a spiritual field and, like a fish in the water, we didn't notice the difference. But as we arrived at the base of the mountain, where the world was humming in agitation, I realised that I was in a special state. I was in a state of communion with God that had been offered to me by Shiva at that time. I was so amazed at this feeling and so fascinated that, then too, I prayed to God to always keep me in that state. I tried staying awake for as long as I could. I feared that if I fell asleep I would lose it. I enjoyed this special communion with God till the morning, when I fell asleep. But being in that state, a special experience happened in the astral plane too. I saw my descent to the physical plane, how I consciously chose to reincarnate, how I chose everything related to the physical appearance of my body, myhouse and the mother that gave birth to me.

It's not a coincidence that I experienced all this over there because of the deep connection with what Arunachala is and the legend of that mountain.

Only there, triggered by the pilgrimage in India and the meditations I did, but mostly because of that special place, I experienced the same state that I had been living in for months.

After eight months, Christmas came and I thought that out of respect, I should undertake a meditation with our Lord Jesus and thank Him for bringing me to God.

I did the meditation and Jesus appeared smiling and reassured me that He is watching over me.

That was all. Then again, for a long period of time, God was the only one in my mind and in my heart. He was the object of my meditation.

During that time, God bestowed His Light upon me continuously. I felt that Light as a state of Grace and Bliss.

Throughout that time, He let that Light be seen. One day, I was walking through the forest with my husband. All of a sudden, my husband said: *Stop, don't move!*

I stopped and he took a picture of me and then showed me what he had captured: a cone of light was shining upon me.

I felt the Light coming down on me all the time. I knew about it so seeing the Light did not surprise me. I was surprised that God wanted it to be seen.

THE LAUGHING FLOWER

When this obsessive period settled down, God started to teach me things about Himself. How He is, what He wished from me and from others. He started to show me, to talk to me and to give me examples. New experiences appeared in my life, experiences of unimaginable beauty.

Worried, I once prayed for the planet. I was praying that wars would stop and any disaster that might destroy the planet and humanity would be avoided. The mass media was littered with all sorts of news about disasters, be it a comet, an earthquake or maybe that a war was about to start. It was 2012 and the end of the world was said to be imminent - no matter the year. People were afraid and concerned, and some groups were meditating and praying for the planet to be saved.

That concern got to me and I started a series of prayers. It was a certain type of prayer and it was necessary to stand facing east.

On the same day, I received a beautiful bunch of flowers and I offered them immediately to Jesus. I then placed them under a panting of Jesus.

I was standing in front of that painting, praying.

At some point, I opened my eyes and I saw one of the flowers, a gerbera. Something made me look at it. Under my eyes the flower transformed:

Eyes appeared on it, then a small nose, then a big laughing mouth. The eyes were directly watching me and through them, it transmitted a cosmic laughter. All the Universe was laughing, everything was shaking from that laughter and so was my body. Every cell was laughing.

Simultaneously I received a message from God, telling me *not to worry because He will take care of everything.*

I felt His fatherly love for each one of us and His constant and continuous care. God is watching over us in every moment. We are carried in His hands, under His protective wing, in His arms throughevery second of our existence.

More than that, He is not abandoning us, He is not punishing us and He won't end the world.

He created this Universe, which is functioning according to certain Laws. The Law of Cause and Effect is the one creating tensions and karmic burnings at different moments in time. We get scared and we think the end of the world is coming.

The end of the world is not coming.

Fear gets to those who have lost their faith and then they spread the word about the end.

The world itself is God and God is endless.

This is the illusion of eternity – we believe that the transient things are eternal and we can't see the eternity that belongs to God and to our spirit, which is a part of God.

God was amused by my fear and as a loving father or a tender lover, He told me not to worry about His work.

It would be best if once and for all we would end all these fears and enjoy the Marvellous World that God has created for us. We are living in a paradise and because of the fear of the end, we are not seeing the world for what it is, so we are not able to enjoy it.

When will the time come for us to enjoy this creation of God? Will it ever come?

We keep running all day long, we victimise ourselves, we are afraid, we want to save the planet… But, my dear reader, have you seen how wonderful this planet that you inhabit actually is? Have you made the time to see it, to visit it, to enjoy it or are you too preoccupied with saving it?

I think that many of you will contradict me and call me ignorant.

What I am telling you is that each of us can 'save' the planet if, from where we are, we become a little better, be more patient, lend a helping hand to those in need. If we offer our shoulder to anyone who may need it to cry on, if we take care of a plant or an animal, etc.

It is said that this blue planet is a planet of love. Then let's offer our love to it! The planet suffers because of the lack of love. How should we love it? By looking at its picture and saying that we are transmitting our love when we don't know what love is? How can I transmit something that I don't know? We should start with those who are near us before aiming so far. We need to learn what unconditional love is and we need to bring it into our lives. Let's unconditionally love our families, our neighbours, the people that we comein contact with, the strangers, the places that surround us. All of them hold all of God's love: the clouds, the sun, the grass, the flowers, the mountains, the butterflies, the snakes and all living creatures; because God lives in all of them.

We are saving the planet by showing our love, and not just talking about it.

This planet is a planet of love, of the love of God and we took away its love. We don't know what love is anymore.

I once spoke with a couple who was having problems in their relationship and they were asking me: *And what is love precisely?*

We crave love, we desperately ask for it but we are not capable of giving it.

Pardon my question but: *Are you jealous?* I hope you're not.

This is not a sign of promiscuity, but if your lover or husband falls in love with another woman, why aren't you happy for him, if you say you love him? And the reverse, if your girlfriend or wife is falling in love, why would you feel like killing her or divorcing her? This is not love. Let him love! Let her love! Be happy that they can love! Falling in love is a grace. We cannot fall in love at our own will.

Enjoy his joy, enjoy her happiness. Maybe this new love won't end in a relationship and sex; maybe that is not even necessary. But we, if we could, would put a seal on our partner's heart so that they won't be able to love anyone otherthan us.

Does this description resemble you?

There are so many situations in life when love is misunderstood. So many!

We love our child but we don't care about the one sleeping on the streets without any clothes to wear or food to eat.

We share the bed with our cats or dogs and we sterilise the stray ones.

Let's really love and then the planet will certainly be saved.

All the rest we should leave to God.

I felt God's roar of laughter in me when the flower transformed. My whole being was laughing.

I roared in laughter together with God or, I should say, that God was laughing in me. The laughter was in me, all of me was laughing.

I was laughing in a complete state of freedom. I was laughing atthe joy of finally discovering that God takes care of us. That gave me such a feelingof safety, of confidence! I felt safe on this planet, in this Universe.

By understanding that *God takes care of everything,* every trace of concern that resided in me disappeared.

We are under His care. We should trust Him because He is always protecting us from any calamity.

From that point on, I abandoned myself, I let myself into His care. And I did so with the concern for the planet as well- I left it to Him.

I understood then that only a change in our attitudes and behaviours can change everything. It can stop any disaster, any war, any comet or earthquake. We humans are praying, meditating, bringing offerings; we conduct rituals, all in order to avoid a calamity. But when we end our spiritual practice, we become the ones who we were in the beginning: not paying attention to one another, not loving, lacking kindness, altruism and compassion, etc.

It is enough to be good, to care about others, to show compassion, be altruistic, to spread love and then, the entire planet will transform into a garden of flowers. Any calamity can be stopped if we transform our character.

I would say to all those trying to save the planet: transform yourself, be good, open your soul, spread the love, take care of the one next to you, use your mind, your heart and your intuition, don't act robotically and thus you will save the planet a thousand times more.

For about three days I 'roared' in laughter with God, literally and not just metaphorically. All was laughing in me and around me.

This time I experienced God's joy and happiness and I learned that He also has a Godly Sense of Humour.

ASK ME ANYTHING AND YOU SHALL HAVE IT

I started to discover God more and more over the following period. My relationship with Him was developing. His relationship with me started at the beginning of time but I couldn't say that *I* already had a relationship with Him.

I was discovering Him as the days went by.

I was amazed that He was fulfilling my every wish. Once, I said to myself: *Oh Lord, I barely get the chance to do anything for You because You serve me all the time.*

All you did was to keep your promise.

At first, a long time ago, I heard your voice above my head as you told me:

Ask me anything and you shall have it!

Even though I didn't dare believe this back then, it was You. Yes, You Lord!

The second time, as I heard your roars of laughter, you said **not to worry because You will take care of everything**.

And there was also a third time. It was when I ended *tapas* that consisted of visiting and meditating at the twelve Jyotirlinga in India.

These are twelve places where it is said that God left traces of His presence and actions on Earth. Each of these places has its spiritual story or, rather, a spiritual message for humanity. I have also written a book on this subject.

My dilemma about Shiva and God had been resolved, they were the Same, Unique God.

My aspiration of reaching Him, of being one with Him materialised in a physical activity I performed, when I visited all twelve Jyotirlinga in India -the Godly Lights. I meditated there in order to feel Him and receive His spiritual message.

The last one I visited was in Kedarnath, at an altitude of 3583m. I reached it after a few tests and spiritual efforts.

I'll tell you all about it.

I was on a spiritual journey through India with a few friends. We planned to visit some special temples. For me, it was the completion of a spiritual, physical, material and financial effort that had been spread over ten years – going on an initiatory route under the protection and guidance of Lord Shiva and of the liberated Hindu seer, Adi Shankaracharya.

You can complete such *tapas* in just a month, if considered purely from a physical point of view. In India, things happen differently: you cannot go when you want and where you want. India is alive spiritually and that is what makes it so fascinating. It's not your will that you will do there, but God's will. So, you won't go where you want to. The saints and liberated beings, whether incarnated or not, will offer you their spiritual guidance.

So, you can arrive in India as a simple tourist and not know what brought you there. You simply feel a calling that you can't resist, you get your plane ticket, you travel there and you will always arrive exactly where you need to. Every trip to India becomes spiritual, without you even knowing it. It's never by chance you go there. All those who visit it return home transformed. Something has changed in them.

The same happened to us when we travelled there for the first time. It was then that we found out about the existence of the twelve Jyotirlinga. It was only on our second trip that we were able to visit the first of them, the one in Rameshwaram. We visited it as simple tourists because we were still close-minded back then. So we refused any preliminary preparations. In spite of that, Shiva was understanding and gave us the chance to reach the front of the altar easily, without obstruction. Through Shiva's grace we undertook that trip. We meditated there – our first meditation in such a place. As soon as we sat down, we felt the SahasraraChakra opening and we 'saw' the column of Light that united us with the heavens. Simultaneously, I felt a detachment from the physical world and of being united in my heart with God. We were amazed by how quickly these states could be accessed in these places. I promised myself then to visit all twelve Jyotirlinga. I managed to see each of them when I was ready and the path to them was opened. I couldn't force things or plan them.

So, when the time came, I visited the last one on my itinerary, the one in Kedarnath.

Our desire to reachthere was so great that we contacted a travel agent long before our trip there and we booked ahelicopter flight threemonths in advance, to be sure we wouldn't miss getting there. Because of a big flood the previous year, the road to Kedarnath had been destroyed. Many pilgrims died with the flooded area extending all the way to Rishikesh, 100 km away.

The access to the temple had opened again, one year after the flood and we were amongst the first tourists on the list allowed to go there.

This Jyotirlinga was saved through a miracle.

Abundant rainfall caused a dam to fracture up in the mountains and all the water flowed furiously through the valley, taking with it rocks, trees, cars and people. Somehow, a rock stopped right behind the temple, causing the ragingwaters to split into two streams. Thus, the temple was protected.

Saving this sacred place from destruction was a real miracle of Shiva.

Over the next year, with the exception of the winter, when snow would cover everything, they worked to reconstruct the access road.

On the 1st of May of the following year, the access road reopened and we arrived in the area on the 17th. Because the road was still under construction, the only ways to get there were either by foot, on a trail, or by helicopter. The trail that went up there was a long one, needing more than a day to reach the temple, and access to the trail was restricted. Only sadhus were allowed and the few Hindus that were able to prove, through all sorts of papers and approvals, that they were in good health.

All the rest, as long as they had the money to pay for the expensive flight, were brought up there by helicopter. Approvals and medical results were needed for them too.

As we arrived there from Haridwar, we were taken to our accommodation: tents. This was upsetting for a few colleagues from the group. We'd paid a lot for this trip and they must have wanted better accommodation. However, it was evening by then and there was nothing we could have done.

On the way there, we stopped at a medical point to have some tests done and to get the approval for going there. Earlier, in Rishikesh, both the car and the driver were checked. It was a difficult road to Guptkashi, carved into the rock, singlelane, risky and proneto accidents.

One of our colleagues was so upset that he wanted to return to Haridwar immediately. But it was evening, it was getting darker and going back meant sure death.

At 3am, we were woken by noises on the field. People were agitated and were shouting. They disturbed us and our grumpy colleague shouted at them, asking them to quieten down.

We woke up at 7 in the morning and received hot water in a bucket, which became another reason fordiscontent. Then we had breakfast and by 8 o'clock we were ready for the helicopter flight. It was around 9am when we arrived at the departure point for the helicopter and, with certainty, we advanced through the crowd, showing our tickets booked three months in advance to the employees. We believed that all was settled and all we needed to do was to get on the helicopter.

There was a big crowd and everyone also had their tickets for that day. We were sent to the end of the queue by those who had woken up at 3am and were still waiting there. Only a few groups were taken to the temple and then, because of the snow and the winds, the helicopters were stopped. Oops! What were we to do now? We realised then that booking the tickets in advance was of no use. Nobody was moving, all were waiting. We started to meditate, to pray. Only Shiva's grace would have made it possible for us to get up there. Talking with the others around us, we understood that Kedarnath is not a place one can visit in just one day as we had planned to. In order to visit the temple, one needed a few days. There were many people, the helicopters were going up till just 11am and, even if it wasn't snowing, we still had a three-day wait in the queue.

Hmm…what were we supposed to do now? We had reservations in Badrinath for the following day and that was 200km away, on a difficult mountain road, as mentioned before.

It was 11am and we were clearly told that there would be no more flights to the temple that day.

I must admit we were saddened. Unhappy, we went down tothe valley, to Guptkashi, in order to do some shopping. We found a very old temple there, built by the Pandavas when they had travelled around in the region in search of Shiva.

The Mahabharata tells us that following the war in which the Pandavas killed their relatives, they travelled in search of Lord Shiva in order to receive His forgiveness for their crimes. It was a long pilgrimage for them and, from time to time, they believed that they saw Shiva in certain places, from a distance. When they wouldget close, He wouldnot be there. And duringthis pilgrimage of theirs, they arrived here. They were already on the mountain and it seemed to them that they would never find Him. They stayed longer in this place, now named Guptkashi, and they built a temple where they would pray and perform rituals consecrated to Shiva.

They received new signs from Shiva after a period of prayer. They continued their ascent up the mountain till the place where Kedarnath is now. There, Shiva appeared in front of them, blessed them and left a Jyotirlinga.

It was not by chance that we arrived at this temple without prior knowledge. We meditated there and we prayed to Shiva to perform a miracle for us and help us reach Kedarnath.

Gradually, our self-importance as Occidentals, believing we deserved everything, capitulated and beseechingly, we were looking to the mountain in deep humbleness and hope.

Only our grumpy colleague continued to be upset and discontented. Everything is planned and well organised in the Occident. In India, it seemed we were on faith's will and that disturbed him greatly. This lack of understanding made him sick.

We were at the tents, getting some rest, when we heard a desperate shout. Our sick colleague was feeling so poorly that he thought he would die. He was crying for help. Afraid that something might happen to him, we called the doctor. If it had been necessary, we were ready to give up on Kedarnath and take him to the hospital. But still, thiswas India. Who knows what he might have eaten. Maybe it was a virus. While the doctor checkedhim, we waited anxiously in front of the tent. The camp manager was looking at us, laughing.

What's up with him, we all wondered. A person might die and he was laughing. The driver was also in a good mood, as if nothing had happened. We were puzzled.

Finally, the doctor came out and fearful, we asked him what was happening with our colleague. The doctor answered calmly:

- *Nothing.*
- *Nothing? He has fever...almost 40 degrees. He has diarrhoea, nausea, he is vomiting...*
- *There is nothing, he is not sick. It's because of his anger. I gave him an ayurvedic solution, sweet and salty, that he must take every two hours. He needs to go out for walks and not just stay in bed. He will recover quickly.*

The driver started to laugh and the camp manager told us, as politely as he could:

- *You say you booked your helicopter tickets three months ago, but Shiva gives you the tickets to Kedarnath. You'll get there when He wishes, not when you want to. That's why you need at least three days for getting there. Some are waiting for as long as a week. This is an important pilgrimage. When people come here, their mind is set on Shiva. All those who you see here came for this. We've seen a lot. Shiva won't let people arrive at the temple if He doesn't wish it.*

His explanation left us thinking. All of us wanted to go to Kedarnath and we didn't know what else to do but to relent to Shiva.

Early next morning we had to leave forBadrinath, to another Hindu sacred place, the Temple of Liberation. At least we would see that.

But still…we kept thinking… We didn't want to give up.

We told the driver that if it didn't rain the following morning, we'd try once again to get to the temple.

But in the evening, as we went to bed, the clouds gathered, the wind started to blow, shaking the tent, and the rain started.

We looked at one another and sighed. Our chances of getting to Kedarnath were close to zero.

When we woke up in the morning we felt we had to get to the helicopter.

This time, we had woken up early. We didn't care about breakfast. Our colleague quit and the rest of us got into the car and went to the offices where people were assigned for boarding. We were the first ones there. It was pouring down with rain.

After an hour a few other people came, hopeless. The clerks were not there because they knew there was no chance of going up in the rain.

It was around 9am when someone came and told us that we needed to go somewhere else. We went there. People started to gather there too, but not as many. We were told that if the helicopters could fly, we had a chance of getting on one. A glimpse of hope lit our hearts. The rain stopped. We rejoiced. Nobody was moving though. There was snow up in the mountain. After a while, we saw another helicopter coming from Dehradun. It was coming from the valley and it was reserved for the VIPs (Very Important People) and the rich. It was a long distance so the cost of the flight was higherand there were not many who could afford the cost.

- *Look! A helicopter!* we said to the clerks. *If that one can land, then you should let them fly from here too.*
- *Wait, we need to make a phone call.*

They talked on the phone, arranged things and then they took us aside and told us:

- *Pretend you are upset so that the others believe that and go to the other base, where you were before. It will take you from there.*

We hid our joy and proceeded there. They took us from there.

As we got off from the helicopter, we were told that we only had fifteen minutes and then we would need to return.

The time was too short. The walk to the temple was seven minutes each way. We needed time to meditate there too. I decided that I wouldn't leave there without at least fifteen minutes of meditation. I had meditated at every Jyotirlinga and I wanted to do the same here.

The altitude difference made us dizzy. We couldn't breathe properly and we believed we would fall. We started running towards the temple. We figured that as long as we could run, we wouldn't fall.

As we were running, we could see the effects of the previous year's disaster. It was terrible but there was no time for us to look at anything.

Once we arrived at the temple, we realised we had no offerings. Who would've thought about offerings and where to get them from? So we offered our hearts, our souls and all our beings to Shiva. We were impressed with His gift to us – letting us reach there. The priest offered us his blessings and then we found a place in the temple where we started our meditation. It was really cold. It felt like I was sitting on ice. Despite that, I managed to get into a meditative state and was in communion with God. I heard His voice after a little while:

From now on, leave all your worries to me!

At the end of this *tapas*, of this ten-year long effort that cost me thousands of euros, God reassured me once again, for the third time that **I am under His care and all I have to do is to abandon myself**.

After ending this spiritual travel (in May), all the conditions for teaching in India, going on tour there with the theatre (the following year) and writing this book (in November, the same year) were created.

HIS LOVE

We meet different people in life and our interactions are diverse. One of these people has been in my life for years. He was like a brother to me, very close, very understanding and of great help in difficult times. Unfortunately, our relationship had to end at onepoint. We love all the people in our lives; some we love more than others and our love for each person is different. I loved that person too, in a certain way.

Throughout my relationship with Jesus and then with God, he was also there, somewhere. When he left, my soul retained a lot of love that somehow belonged to him. It was a similar situation with the one I told you about before, just that now there was no crisis or sufferance. I was in the hands of God and He took care of me.

Once again, someone had left me and I still had my love for them in my heart, not knowing what to do with it. But then God came, in a state similar to a great absorption, because I don't know how to describe it otherwise, and He told me:

Give it all to Me, give Me all that love!

And He took it, without waiting for me to give it to Him. I felt how all the love I carried in my heart for that person was transferred to Him. He was absorbing it and transforming it into the Love of God. Together with this love, my attachment to that person also went. There were no more regrets, no more questions, no illusions and no more karma that was tying me to him.

As I previously said, once beyond the threshold, God takes you in His hands. He takes care of your karma and burns it instantly, without you having to make an effort. He does it all. You belong to Him once you give yourself completely to God. He will do everything for you.

It's a miracle to be able to see this process from outside. It's like you are watching the film of your life. You witness your existence. It is sublime.

I felt that God was happy and enthusiastic. Yes, I was feeling the states flowing from Him and being transmitted to me afterwards.

I then felt Him as a very masculine man who loved me as though I was the perfect lover. My relationship with Him transformed. I was now His lover and from that point I was not able to name Him my Heavenly Father. He was my Adored Lover.

I understood that in order to be God's lover, you needed to be in love with Him.

And I was.

This made me understand the Shiva aspect of God, that perfect masculine which is the counterpart of Shakti, the perfect feminine. Together they form the Whole.

GOD LOVES US ALL

Experiencing this new love relationship with God, with all its new aspects and emotions, pride started to grow within me. I was proud of being so loved by Him and I would sometimes ask myself why He had chosen to love me so deeply.

Do you feel like laughing? Don't laugh, because God is not laughing at such things. God is never ironic and He never sees one to be better than the other, one as smarter and another asdumber.

With the same love and kindness, He told me:

He loves all in the same way.

And not only that, He also made me feel His love for all, this equal love, a love that sees no differences.

It was such a revelation. He planted this type of love in my heart, equal and unconditional, for all.

Since then, I never saw anyone as being superior to another. All humans are equally precious, no matter whether they are beggars or rich, sick or healthy, good or bad.

God's Love was living in me for all people, allowing me to see their value. And that was the value of their Supreme Self *Atman*.

Among all the gifts I received from Him, this was the most precious one.

I cannot compare anything to the state I feel when I look at someone, no matter who he or she is, and I can see their godly value, their Supreme Self.

Thank You Lord!

Dear readers, this is the reason I wrote this book – *to tell you that God loves you all equally. You are no less than any other human being on this planet or any other spirit created by God. The Divine Spark shines in each of us. God resides in every oneof us. God is equally in each of us. What we see as differences arecreated by our awareness. The 'quantity' of God's love doesn't differ but what is different is the level of our awareness, how aware we are that God resides in us.*

Open the eyes of your soul and see the God in you. Become aware of His presence there. All He is waiting for is to be seen.

Once you see Him, your whole life will change. Like the 'Bhagavat Gita' says, God will come to guide your soul to liberation. He will restrain the horses, He will drive them, He will drive the carriage. From that point on, He will carry you. The moment you recognise Him in you is the moment you will go beyond the threshold. Once there, He does everything for you and for your happiness.

From that point on you will truly be a happy being, forever!

God gave us free will and the chance to choose in every moment. Our everyday choices can transform our destiny. If what we want is to go beyond the threshold, to let God be in charge of our destiny, we need to make some choices, without changing our minds afterwards. We have to choose God every time, every moment and at every turning point.

We have to leave our life, our destiny and our love in His hands.

GOD WANTS ALL OUR LOVE

For many years I loved someone and I was fighting with myself because I didn't want love for a man as I felt it would drive me away from God. Oh, how human our thinking can be!

He then told me:

Love without having any expectations.

And I understood then that when we love someone, it's our expectations that put a distance between God and us. When we give all in that love and we have no expectations, that's when we love Him, who resides in that person.

Thank You Lord!

A CHANNEL FOR THE ONES AROUND ME

This love I felt for God created the context for others, who were in my presence and feeling my state, to experience special spiritual states.

Of course, none of these are owing to my merit. I was just experiencing my state and my friends or the students, who also saw me as a friend, would live similar states.

I met a friend once and we talked about ordinary things. The next night, he had a dream of Jesus. He was so excited to have felt Him. From what he told me, it seemed a real astral meeting. The emotion of that meeting was imprinted on his face and his soul was full of joy and love.

Another time, I taught my students to be divine channels. Some of them felt God and a lady, who loved me profusely, experienced a deep state of *Samadhi*.

On another occasion, during a class, we did a meditation, as a present for a girl who was celebrating her birthday. God offered me the state of equality in love during that meditation, at the same time gifting me the experience of ideal love. I was simultaneously completely detached from those there and loving the totality. Some of the students loved me more, others loved me less, but through God's Grace I was able to feel His equal love for all of them. These Divine gifts are for all and are bestowed upon all of us, but being aware of them is directly proportional with the openness of our souls. The one to whom that gift was offered told us, with tears in her eyes, that she felt bliss and eternity. I closed my eyes and I felt I was becoming a column united with the heavens. I understood then that the girl had the experience of the Divine Ecstasy, *Samadhi*. All the students in the hall were delighted and happy. Nobody was envious. Amongst them existed a sublime state of love and wonder.

Another time, once again during a class, I experienced *Samadhi*. When the meditation ended, the same girl told me about the state she had experienced. It was again a state of divine ecstasy, only this time it had been more profound and it had transformed her.

I was aware that all of these were God's gifts.

Once, I performed an unconventional treatment for an eighty-eight-year-old man. The procedure took just a few minutes. After I finished, the man stood up and he was impressed. With emotion in his voice he told me that the heavens had opened, a golden light had come down on him and he heard God's voice.

I want to explain something now – when you hear God's voice or when you see His Light or any other form in which He chooses to be seen, you are actually feeling more than you are seeing. You can feel His love, His unlimited kindness, His perfection, His friendship, His protection... You are then able to feel all the qualities in their absolute form.

During the course I am teaching, about the happiness of discovering God, the students are able to feel Him and they are amazed to see how close He really is.

SHIVA AND PARVATI

I was experiencing that state of being God's Lover with such intensity that during that precise time, a director offered me the part of Parvati in a theatre show. There was not much that I had to do. I had to go on stage at a certain time and perform a *mudra*. I got on the stage, representing Her, and the public felt Her Manifest through my being. The prolonged applause acknowledged me.

God was acting as being in love. Actually, it is said that He is really in love with His creation. He was offering me gifts, offerings, surprises, including the acting part I had received.

As I was preparing for the show, I suddenly felt I was in love with Shiva.

He loved me as Jesus, He loved me through the Angels and now He was loving me as Shiva.

It's true that throughout my travels and my studies related to India, I felt I had loved Shiva, but there's a difference between loving and being in love.

One day, as I was gazing with admiration upon the image of Parvati, Shiva's consort, I uttered a prayer:

Help me to be as beautiful as You are, and help me to love Shiva like You love Him.

As though She heard my prayer, soon after I felt I was in love with Shiva.

Then I felt His love and, more than that, I felt Him looking atme as His beloved wife.

What am I saying? All of us, women, are Parvati. It's just that we don't realise it in the beginning. If only we knew, our lives would be different.

Women are so dependent on signs, on compliments, on attention, on a smile from a man. They are always searching for the Ideal Lover.

He exists since the beginning of time; we just need to open our eyes and our hearts to see him.

After I received the part, my husband came home and told me: *We are going to India!* He suddenly felt an urge to go there on a spiritual trip.

Oh, what a surprise! *Shiva, You're calling me close to You? In Your country, in Your house? In Your temple?*

Thank You, my adored lover! Thank You Shiva!

I always said that these states are not imaginary because they reverberate in all the material world.

Any real state of communion with God will be felt all the way to the physical plane.

SOLITUDE

I felt Him looking at me as beautiful woman, gifted with many qualities.

I discovered myself as a woman during that time. I regained my confidence, I saw my value.

God restored my status of a Complete Being, of a special woman. He showed me my potential and helped me to succeed in all that I started. He opened my eyes to allow me to see myself, to know myself better and to appreciate myself.

I was living in a world where love and happiness was all there was. I wasn't touched by this world, or by frustration and discontent. It took me some time till I learned how to bring the upper world down here. At first, you feel torn from the world you are living in. But then, after you learn a few lessons directly from God, you can bring that Paradise to earth and share it with others.

There was a time when I wanted to give, I wanted to give myself, but the world I was living in rejected me. Who was I to teach them? Really, who was I? Nobody.

A period of forced isolation followed. I was somehow rejected by the society in which I had lived till then because I had become different and I was experiencing states of communion with God that were not approved by them.

But I was prewarned about this period. As I was meditating on New Year's Eve, I heard God telling me:

From now on you are on your own!

Oh God, what are you saying?! I'll take anything, but don't leave me!

What was God trying to tell me?

He was right, as always. It was just a loving notice of what was to come in my life, so I wouldn't be surprised and shocked by it.

Two months after receiving that message I was excluded from the spiritual society I was living in. The society was my life. I had friends there, I was expressing myself artistically, spiritually, physically in that community. For over twenty-five years, my life had beenthere. Without being aware of it, I was living in a bubble, believing that society to be the best place to be in the world, totally rejecting the outer world.

I didn't want to leave it, but God helped me. I thought that all the beautiful, kind and spiritual beings are there. And that was false.

Expanding my consciousness, God removed me from the bubble so I could see beauty and perfection in all human beings.

There is no point in repeating the story; I already told you in one of the chapters before about how this world left my life.

What I want to underline now is that if we live in illusion, God will take us out of it. Once we are in God's heart, nothing ever happens without us being warned and helped.

Under normal circumstances, an event like this would crush a person, but God helped me get over it easily, offering me much more than I had lost.

I was harshly judged by my best friends who, at that point, were saying that I was drifting from the path. The illusion is so big! The moment you are better anchored in God, some would say you are lost.

I told them then: *Ask God and He will tell you the Truth.*

I've seen God answering all those who believe in Him. It's as simple as that - just ask Him. God will answer all your questions.

My response to my friendscausedeven greater effectsand I was asked:

- *Do you think God answers you when you want?!*

Oh, yes. He is so close. Only a blind person couldn't see this closeness.

Ask Him. Talk to Him. Dare to believe that He is listening toyou and He willanswer you *every time.*

Apparently, I was alone because those who were my friends, those I was counting on, rejected me. But God never left me. He was with me all the time and compensated that loss through His gifts. So, I was never really alone.

That time was like going back to school for me. Till then I had beencounting on other people's decisions and approvals. From that point on I had to learn to have faith in God's help, in my communication with Him, in His signs. It was like starting from scratch. But I couldn't stop. I went forward, having complete faith in God, permanently feeling His love and guidance.

It was a transforming process. A base was destroyed and another one, a more solid one, was built in its place.

Lord, what would I do without You?

DEPENDENCE

Sometimes, an immense silence surrounded me... There was nobody I could talk to about God, and other subjects were of no interest to me.

I totally trusted God and I knew that every word He was saying to me was true. I was connected to Him. Like a plug in a power socket...and the socket was God. Everything was common sense, humanity, love and harmony... This spiritual evolution is not a big deal. If you respect the rules that make you Human, you are already a spiritual being.

There were times when I felt the need to share my experiences with someone, to talk about them. As soon as I brought up the subject it was like everybody knew everything about it and they preferred to talk about something else, like ordinary life subjects – where have you been, what else have you done, what did you eat, what movies have you seen, have you heard about this or that...etc. Whenever I tried telling them that there is more to life than just that, everyone knew everything and I rarely got a chance to meet someone who would gladly talk about God.

All I wanted to talk about was Him and often doors were closed in my face. That taught me to remain in silence but my soul was saddened because people were refusing to understand that God is everything and without Him you are nothing.

More than that, the ones who rejected me from the society I was living in till then ironically said that I live in an imaginary world whenever I tried to tell them something about faith and God. I must admit that a part of my soul was sad. I was amazed to realise that those who spoke so beautifully about God werenot able to feel Him.

In such a moment of sadness, God told me:

Why would you care about getting other people's attention when you have Me and I am offering you all My attention?

It was like a cold shower. It was like God had told me: *Wake up!What are you waiting for from them? I am here with you, isn't My presence making you happy?*

In other words, He gave me the strength to detach myself, to turn my back and leave.

He was so right! He was with me all the time, giving me all of His attention and often, I was not able to benefit from His Grace because I was waiting for some attention from otherpeople.

How lovingly He told me that! And God, how happy we would be if we did turn our attention towards Him!

This is how I learned to detach from people and their opinions.

When His love and attention were overwhelming me, I would say – *God, what would I be without you?* I was grateful and I realised that I couldn't live without His love.

The love in my heart was so big that, at times, I felt it was suffocating me, burning me. Sometimes I was unable to do anything, I wouldjust sit there, inert, because I was beyond my physical body.

I was love, I was breathing love. At the same time love was flowing towards and from me.

LESSONS

One day I decided to grasp a meditation of communion with God and I felt I would like it to be the most powerful meditation ever. I thought I'd use a **mantra**and from all the initiations I had received, I felt the one of **Kalki Avatar**would be the most appropriate.He must have the most powerful resonance with God since he will be the next reincarnation of the Divine Being.

Shortly after I started to meditate, I heard God telling me in a kind and amused tone:

Now you want to squeeze Me into a mantra?

My mind froze. I realised how right He was. What name or sequence of letters could comprise Him?! He is more than that, much more. He is everything and this part expresses just one of His aspects.

On the other hand, by being in direct communion with Him, I was able to feel the real value of the Kalki Avatar mantra that I had received. God took me to the essence of this mantra and it was clear to me how this mantra couldtake each devotee towards communion with Kalki Avatar.

But in the mantra,it's just Kalki and not God in his entirety.

I thanked Him for talking to me again. I had beenmissing His voice. When He talked to me He was leading me to the essence and He was planting that truth in my being. I felt all

His love, kindness, greatness. He was eager to teach me, He was understanding aboutmy inabilities and ignorance and He was never a harsh judge.

Actually, I never felt Him upset with me or others. The idea the God could be upset with us is one of the greatest illusions that mankind created.

Through the lessons that He offered me with so much kindness, lessons that came together with real examples, I was able to understand that God is actually our true guide. He always was and He always will be.

But we are not ready to receive the teachings directly from Him. So there appears the need for loving and self-sacrificing human beings to teach us.

What are we missing in order to always be in communion with God?

It's just our desire to be.

God had a lot of work to do on me till I learned that He gave us everything and we are entitled to enjoy this abundance and plenitude. In today's society, spirituality is associated with asceticism and people have the tendency to think that as long as you enjoy life, you are not spiritual.

The moment I gave everything up and I offered myself to Him completely, He gave me everything and more. I gave up on all that was mine and,in exchange, He gave me all that was His, which is so much more.

He was patient with me till I learned it.

He taught me to do treatments accompanied by the Archangel Raphael. I was already a therapist and in order to do my work, I would pray to Archangel Raphael to send to me all those He wanted to cure alongwith me. Then, when the patients arrived, I would invitethem to my practice and ask Archangel Raphael to do His work as I was doing mine. The patients were rapidly healed and it often surprised me that after only a few sessions they were healthy.

It was actually Archangel Raphael who was doing His work. The patients didn't return after they were healed because there was no need for them to do so.

I was praying one evening for a relative to be cured. Subsequently, during the night, whenI was sleeping, a healing method was revealed to me and I used if for that person. In the morning, he was completely cured.

That healing method is based on relaxation. A sick organ, member or body can be healed instantly if it relaxes completely. In the astral plane, during sleep, I induced this state of relaxation inthe sick person and that made the healing possible inthe morning.

It is a method that is worth remembering: the body will heal if we relax it profoundly.

Another time I was asked to go see a sick person and performa treatment. It was a child. She was in a crisis and instead of taking her to the doctors, the parents brought her to me. I was not at home at that time but later, when they eventually contacted me by phone, they asked if I could come totheir house.

The child had digestive problems: fever, chills, diarrhoea, vomiting. As I headed there, I prayed to God: ***Lord, what can I do for her? You heal this child because it is in Your power to do that!***

I performed a healing technique for her so that the parents wouldn't say that I came there and did nothing. They needed to see me doing something for her. But all my hope and faith was in God.

As I left, I told them that she wouldbe alright.

I trusted that and God had already confirmed it. And so it was.

I left the girl in a state of deep sleep. She woke up the next day, cured.

Another time, He taught me that there is nothing wrong in asking for money and welfare (from Him) because it is similar to asking for water and food.

This helped me understand that it is natural to live well in this thriving world, full of God's gifts. The world around us thrives in gifts, all created for us.

Another important lesson was when God told me:

I desire to live your life.

I had a dilemma. My problem seemed too small to 'bother' God with it.

It was then thatI felt Him telling me, lovingly and compassionately, that *nothing is too small and insignificant for Him*. At the same time, He let me know that it is His desire and pleasure to get involved in all the activities in our life, to realise them together with us and even to live our life.

I felt then how present He really is in our lives and how He is living life through us.

Since then, His presence in my actions, in my life was very clear to me. Many times, I would feel the flavour of His presence in me and, as I evolved, I realised things and actions with His hands, or to put it in a better way, He realised them through me.

Another time He said:

There is nothing you need to do, as you are, you are perfect…you are Whole…

I sat on a chair upon hearing that and I enjoyed the message that I had received. This has been another exemplification: He made me feel perfect as I am because His entire presence exists in me.

Meanwhile, the Universal Being had awakened in me. I was not just what I saw in the mirror. So I was feeling perfect as I was, no matter the colour of my skin or of my eyes, no matter the level of my intelligence, my studies or my titles or if my physical shape was perfect or not, or if I was healthy or sick.

Nowadays, people waste a lot of time and energy on their appearance, on how they are seen by others, without seeing their real reflection - which is God.

THE COURSE

In this way, God taught me many lessons and He is still teaching me, even today. Part of those learnings will be described in the next chapter.

One day He asked me to start a class where I would teach others to love Him as I did. I froze.

Oh Lord, why are You asking me to do that? How will I do it?

Doubt crept into my mind about whether I was the right person to deliver this course. What would I say to the people? And to whom? Where wouldI find the students?

God insisted.

I thought it was just my imagination, so I asked for a clear sign from God, to be sure it wasHis Will to start this course.

It was past midnight and I was returning home on a train. The train started in Budapest and was almost empty. I was alone in the coach.

About sevenminutes after I had asked for the sign, a lady came towards where I was seated. She was the waitress from the restaurant coach. She was Hungarian and didn't speak Romanian or English.

She approached me and gave me a Catholic rosary. It was an old one, silver with pearls. She probably gotit from her mother or grandmother. I could tell it was important toher by the way she held it. She spoke just one word to me, probably the only word she knew in Romanian - *Îngeri (Angels)* - and then she gestured so that I would understand that it was a gift for me, from the Angels.

I was perplexed and I wanted to refuse it because I could see how dear the rosary was to her. But through her gestures she insisted and then she took my hand and placed it on the rosary. After that she left.

, I was alone once again in that train racing through the night. I was looking at the rosary. It was well worn from constant prayer and I understood then that it was the sign I had asked for.

In the night, in that empty train, God found a person to be the instrument for His answer! It was amazing how He did it. It was not a dream, it was real. The rosary I was looking at was the sign I had requested. God found that big-hearted person to manifest His answer through her.

After a while, I went in search of the woman. It was then that I saw that the coach was empty and that the next coach was the restaurant and the lady was serving there. But she had no clients. That coach was empty too.

I ordered some food. I wanted to talk with hera bit. But there was no way to do that. I couldn't speak Hungarian and she couldn't speak Romanian. Either way, she didn't want to talk. She hadfulfilled hermission.

That answer convinced me and I decided to start the course.

But how would I do it? What would I say to the people?

I asked God and He answered:

Follow your steps!

I read my journal. It was not clear to me as tohow all the spiritual events had happened in my life. It was true that I meditated and prayed a lot, but it never seemed enough.

I decided to listen to God and to start the course.

I let some of my friends know that I would be teaching this course and they showed interest init. I was being shown how God was choosing and then sending the students inthe way the first lot of them appeared.

He also showed me how to structure the classes.He decided there would be tenclasses, one for each step towards the communion with Him, and a maximum of ten people in each class. Each step was based on the previous one so it was important not to miss any of the classes. Anyone unable to attend a class was not allowed to attend the subsequent classes. The classes would be once a week and there would be homework. God gave me the guarantee that people would get to feel Him and to communicate with Him at the end of the course. He also told me what the fee should be. It was not too high. It was actually less than other similar ones in the market. He also gave me important information that was helpful for me as a teacher.

The first class was close and I still had no idea what I would talk about. Then He inspired me and I wrote. Each time, before the class, God would dictate the text and He would tell me what to teach them. I wrote these courses under His direct guidance.

God spoke through me and I said what people needed to hear, at the precise time. All of them felt God's presence. All of them saw how easy it was to create a relationship with Him. They learned to love Him, to be in love with Him. Their lives changed for the better. They became new people.

Every day they had homework to do. The ones who did their homework deepened their relationship with God. The ones who forgot to do it, were drifting apart.

God created a very short and easy path towards Him through this course.

I feel a strong drive from Him, each time I start a course. He chooses the right time to start each program.

Each time, together with the students, I experience special states. I always thank them for giving me the opportunity to teach it (the course).

HOW GOD IS

Whenever I thought about God or whenever I would see or feel Him, He was perfection in all possible aspects.

He is love, joy, fulfilment, plenitude, abnegation, satisfaction, love… There is no trace of the smallest crack or resonance with something negative.

Then why do people see Him differently? They believe God is testing them, is punishing them, is not paying attention to them, is not listening to their prayers. They believe He is judging them and that He is upset with what they do… What made them acquire this distorted belief?

On different occasions, there were problems I needed to sort out. As usual, I would prepare to pray for God's help. But as soon as I thought about Him I would feel Him in all of His perfection and plenitude; my problem was not a part of that perfect harmony.

I was trying to tell Him: *God, this is serious,* but everything remained unchanged in His perfection.

Whenever I ran to Him with a problem, He showed me that there was none. All was as clear and serene as the summer sky. My problem wouldn't fit inside Him. Actually, it never existed. As a proof of that, although it seemed very difficult, it was immediately sorted.

I was therefore living in a continuous awareness of His presence next to me. Previously, I would have said I lived in a continuous communion with Him.

Yes, all of us are completely united with Him, permanently. We understand this based on our level of awakening. I mean that even though we experience permanent states of 'communion with Him', states of ecstasy, of boundless love, of adoration, only later I realised that being in communion with Him means something else.

ALWAYS IN LOVE

Feeling His presence next to me, I had no desire to ask for anything because I felt I had everything. There was no drive to realise something, to attain something... I felt I had everything and there was nothing more I could wish for.

The most beautiful thing in my life was the love I felt for Him and I feel that even now.

I was in love with Him and I am in love with Him now too.

In this private, intimate relationship with Him, I addressed Him as a Lover and He would answer me in the same way.

Sometimes I would write rhymes to Him, other times letters and on other occasions, I wrote in my journal as though I was speaking to Him.

THE LOVE FOR GOD

I was addressing God with a lot of love in my prayers. Knowing Him so close to my heart, the formal expressions disappeared.

The idea is that we are always communicating with Him, in every possible way.

Here are some of my prayers:

- *Lord, show me the way. I do so many things but I don't know which of them are right. I do many of them because this is how I my concept of right, but is that Your Will too? Please, send me signs and help me understand what You wish me to do. I promise I'll do what You wish, just help me hear You. Talk to me, Lord!*
- *Please help me, my adored lover!*
- *Please help me amplify more and more and more my love for You. You are always on my mind but I feel there can be more. Please help me love You as much as it is possible, to reach that point where there is no more love left that's not for You. Please God, I beg you with all my being - help me reach that state and let it be with me for all eternity. Even if I have to reincarnate, let me have that state awakened in me. Please God...*
- *Adored lover, love of my life, my soul... I was about to drift away from you without even noticing it, maybe even broke my promise to you but you reminded me about what I had forgotten. Thank You, Lord... The thing is that I don't*

need anyone else to be happy and fulfilled. You give me everything.

For the sake of other people, I want to make a compromise, believing I can offer them love and happiness. But the time for that has not come yet... I cannot get out of You for others.

You offered me all the fulfilments in the world. What more can I wish for?

My adored Lover, I want to ask you something: I live in this plenitude and I'm in a good place, but is it just for myself? Teach me what to do.

- *My adored God, we have a lot to talk about today.*

I want to put things in order in my life and I need your help to clearly understand some aspects. We haven't spoken for a long time and there are certain aspects of my life that I haven't understood lately.

*Please give me the strength to speak with You today because in this heat (*I was in India at that time and the temperatures were really high) *it's difficult for me to function.*

I love you and I will love you for all the days that I live and even beyond life, beyond eternity. My love is Yours forever.

I'll first create an Appendix for this journal about my plans for the future because everything, really everything in my life I want to do with You and not without You.

The richness of my communion with You can be so fulfilling that I wouldn't want anything else. What should I pursue? What else should I wish for? I have You and that's enough. You offer me everything, absolutely everything! I live in this state day by day, moment after moment, why should I struggle? All I can wish now is to fulfil Your Will.

- *Lord, I am longing for you... How much longer will it take for me to completely melt in Your Light? Completely, without any trace of ego, of Semida, of anything from my past lives, to dissolve completely into You! My adored Lover, how longshould I wait? Every moment You come to me with so much love! You offer me everything in this world... Every moment seems like I am in paradise. Thank you for all this well being and this beauty. But help me to be useful, to help others, manifest Yourself through me Lord... I'm in a good place, I experience the good things You placed on this earth. I have the courage to feel good, without thinking of the end of the world, without thinking of disasters, of evil, of sickness. I have the courage to live free and happy in the Garden of Paradise, in the garden You created for our joy and happiness.*

Please give me the strength and courage to talk about this here, in this world where all the others see just disasters and fail to see the beauty You created. They are waiting, fearful of the end of the world. But this end will never come because You are endless. Lord, open their eyes to see Your beauty, to see Your kindness, to see Your love, Your true face, charming and full of Light!

Lord, give me the strength to write about this, to tell the world about this. To let You write through me, to let you transmit what you desire to humanity, to Your Creation, to Your Beauty.

LETTERS

- *In the silence of my heart I am waiting for you, my Lord. Around me there is so much silence and I need You so much! What should I do to find You, because You have something, Your essence…and I need it in order to live. In what language should I speak to You so that You hear me? How many hours, days, months do I have to wait till You'll receive me completely in Your heart? Until You will accept me in Your life? What should I do to please You? I am trembling as I wait for a sign from You. If a little while passes without a sign from You, I wither. When You talk to me, I bloom and flourish. Have You any idea how much I love You? You have something there for me, all for me, something that suits me perfectly, but in order to reach that I have to do something to please You. But what is that? Tell me. I crave so much to know it. I need to know it because without You my life has no purpose. I cannot live my life without You. Welcome me into Your house or Your garden. I would even stand at Your gate if I could see You from time to time…to just get a look from you or even a smile.*

    Can You hear me? Am I speaking loud enough for You to hear me?

    Why do our lives include suffering, can't all sufferings be removed? Lord, I don't want to suffer anymore, I don't want my soul to ache again, I don't want to be lacking anything anymore… You gave me everything except You.

You have always kept your word... Whenever You told me something, so it was... You chose me to be Your fond lover... but to whom should I tell that, who would believe it? And why should I tell anyone, really? I feel so good under Your protection and love. What else could I ask for? You give me everything... my Beloved... Who could understand our love?

You did as You promised... I didn't even notice it, I've just seen your gifts and I rejoiced...

I love You with all my being! I am in love with You and I will always be!

My adored God, You are Yourself a miracle!

Your Love and Grace embrace me all the time... It is not drops but rivers of grace that you pour over me... Lord, how many gifts, how many surprises... You are everything and I am your beloved.

• *You took me under Your care.*

Today I was thinking that I haven't spent time with You lately and I was feeling distant, But You, my dear, You don't mind that negligence of mine. You are the One that will never put any distance between us... Today You filled all my being with love and I experienced the Divine Eros. My heart is full of love, my heart is full of this erotic pleasure of my union with You... You showed me the Divine Lover in You.

...Shortly before this state (a state of Cosmic Orgasm) appeared, I wrote the following:

In the silence of your heart, in the loneliness of your soul you meet God who is planting in your heart an endless spring of happiness.

Once God plants that spring there it is of no importance what your body will do.

You will then feel that God loves you so much that nothing bad can ever happen to you; you feel that all the world is a gift for you... and when you have it all... what else is there to wish for?

And all comes from Him, without you making the smallest effort.

- *Lord, my Beloved, without You I wouldn't rest even for a second in this world... But I wouldn't want to be without You not even for a moment... I love You Lord with all my being...and the entire essence of my existence is my love for You ....*

- *You are my adored Lover, You are my Heart, my Soul, my Breath... I love You Lord, I love You with all my being!*
  My heart is full of love for You...
  I adore You, I love You and I give myself completely to You!

- *I know You create everything, I know You are everything - any thought, any idea, any action, any deed, any state -You are all of these. Then, where am I? I don't exist...even I am You. My adored Lover...*

- *I thank You for existing and for loving me so much every moment, second after second!*

- *I love You with all my being and I believe this is the supreme spiritual practice! Thank You Lord for existing, thank You Lord for awakening this love in me!*

- *My Beloved, I thank You for all Your gifts. You give me the whole world... You give me the infinite, You offer me eternity! You inspire me and You whisper to me, telling me what to do... You work through me... Lord, I am so grateful for that!*

- *You want to keep our relationship secret...so be it Lord! As long as You hold me in Your arms that is good enough for me... I wouldn't want anything else... All I want is You! Why should others come and step on our love? They don't know what we are living and they don't see it even when it is obvious. But that is not important, why should I bother? We are enough for one another... I can feel Your embrace in me... I feel You inside me and outside of me... I feel Your attention and endless love for me and that is enough.*

- *I love You! I love You! I love You! My Lord, my adored! Please keep me on Your path, even though apparently, I am not on any path.*

- *My adored Lover, I love You with all my being! Anything can change but my love for You has no end. Anything can happen to me but my love for You will remain! My Beloved, my flesh is burning with love for You, my mind is always with You, I gave You my heart, my soul is Yours! All that I am is Yours. My love, I love You, I love You, I love You! Teach me how to count to infinity and I will tell You that I love You infinite times!*

- *My adored God, thank You for everything, from the bottom of my soul. And special thanks for answering me today - to an important question I asked You: if love is enough to reach You...and You said IT IS!*

   In my heart, I felt a yearning to be with You and I meditated, evoking the love I felt for You. That was early in the morning when my yearning for You woke me up. Then I slept for a while more. I entered ecstasy in my sleep and You showed me that I can easily reach this state If I realise a certain invocation for others and not for myself.

   Falling asleep with this state of love and giving myself to You, You surprised me with this gift, this state of ecstasy that made me feelsomething similar to fainting.

- *My adored Lord, I feel so tired, it is so late but I don't want to sleep until I write to You - that I love You now more than in every moment of my life.*

- *You know Lord, if I were alone in the Universe I wouldn't feel lonely because I am with You... I thank You for this.*

- *I can feel Your Happiness penetrating my heart...that Happiness without an object that makes me happy...*

- *My Lord, You are my relief and my comfort! It is hard to find someone I could talk to in this world... But You talk to me all the time and you comfort my soul.*

- *Whenever I wake up from my sleep, be it morning or night, my heart is full of love and gratitude for You. It is like in my sleep I am travelling to this secret place where all that there is pure love. This secret place is my heart, where You reside. Love springs from there. It's Your love, my Lord. Then my heart is singing hymns of praise to You. There is so much gratitude in my soul and all I can say is: Thank You Lord that You exist!*

RHYMES

- *What use is there for my eyes if they cannot see You?*
  What use is there for my hands if they cannot touch You?
  What use is there for my lips if they cannot kiss You?
  All my life is nothing but a hymn of praise for You…

- *Just You and me, the supreme mystery,*
  Only we know the secret,
  Only between us the silence talks.

- *I can give up on the entire world, but I can't give up on You*
  I can give up on the air that I breath, but I can't give up on You
  If You are here, then all is well.
  If You are present, then all is well.
  I can't wish for anything without You
  Because nothing exists
  Without You.

- *Everything is You,*
  My being is You,
  How will I be
  Me without You?!

- *To the mysterious place of our heart I ran,*
  To the mysterious place of our meeting I ran,
  Like a lover crazy in love with her Beloved.

137

- *Gone is the day,*
  Done are the chores,
  And now, just You and me.
  Let's have a party!

- *Lord, you chose me,*
  And I chose You.
  What a fortunate choice!

- *I am floating in an ocean of You,*
  From every direction You come towards me,
  From every direction You penetrate me,
  My omnipresent Lover
  You touched my most profound depths
  You deepen in me and you sprout from me.
  ...
  My lips cannot utter "I love You" anymore
  Because not even a thousand "I love yous"
  Could be a measure of my love for You
  ...
  You are playing, hiding Yourself in me
  And I find You each time,
  But that is not enough
  And again I find you,
  And once again,
  And one time more and,
  Still, it's not enough
  ...
  Lord, for once satisfy me!
  I cannot bear absorbing You continuously
  And still be thirsty for You!

- *My life is a stage for Your delight*
  You dance and You party
  ... and I do it with You,
  I dance and I party...
  A continuous soiree...

A continuous wedding
Our wedding!

- *My beloved, can someone be more in love than this?!*

- *In my heart You planted*
  The flower of Happiness.
  I cannot find it anywhere else
  But there, where You,
  Skilled gardener,
  You always make it bloom.

- *Every moment of my life is You*
  In the most mysterious part of my heart
  I meet You!
  The deepest silence
  Tells me the most…
  Every moment of my life is a step towards You.
  You say You'll give me all I'm asking for.
  And here it is, I want You, always and forever.
  Dissolved in You, in Your Light
  So no trace of me is left anymore,
  Humankind won't know of my existence.
  I want to be melted in You,
  To disappear in You… I pray.

  My heart is filled with You
  And so be it!

- *I am so obsessed with You,*
  That I can no longer see,
  I can no longer hear…
  It's like I'm mad…about You.

- *I fly to You,*
  I fly with You,
  I fly through You!

- *As I close my eyes*
  Your world disappears
  And Your world appears.
  When I open my eyes
  Your world disappears
  And Your world appears!

- *Like a child, impatiently waiting*
  For the promised toy,
  I am waiting for the night hours
  When there is just me and You!

  Happiness is not letting me sleep
  When I am in your arms,
  The moon rises and sets
  As I dive into Your embrace.
  ...
  I feel I am loved
  As no one else on earth!
  ...
  ...It's true what they say:
  Whoever feels Your love,
  Can fly on the wings of happiness!
  ...
  I haven't touched the ground for a long time...

- *I cherish every moment of my life,*
  Because I am with You...
  Every moment of my life is You,
  I am endlessly in love with You!

- *Lord, thank You for everything...*
  But mostly for
  Teaching me to love You.

- *My greatest joy,*
  Is You, my Lord!

- *You've found the path, you say?*
  I say that, in fact,
  He found the path
  to You...

- *By creating me*
  You've shown me how much You love me.

- *There is no nobler purpose in life than loving You!*
  That suffices me for being eternally happy.
  My wealth is the love I have for You.
  It is my life.
  It is my reason forbeing.
  I love You...
  Since I have fallen for You
  Any other love is pale...
  Nothing can shine as bright as the emotion
  I feel for You.
  My adored lover,
  Don't ask me not to love You,
  And don't ask me not to be.
  I fell in love with You
  For all eternity.

  ...And the longing that accompanies fulfilment,
  And Your presence...
  My beloved,
  In every moment I miss you,
  In every moment You fulfil me.
  In every moment I'm thirsty for You,
  In every moment you quench my thirst.
  I am hungry and You are feeding me
  with You, Whole You.

  But I, am I, this grain of sand,
  Offering you enough fulfilment?
  Are you contemptuous of me?

Do I offer You enough?
Do I make You happy?

Ask me anything, anything my Love
And, as much as I can, with what I am,
I'll offer you!

As I said this I abandoned myself in Your love...

And Your answer was:
Let go my love, abandon yourself in My waves!
I'll take you to the depths and to the heights,
I'll fly with you and I'll embrace you always!
My love, can't you feel My arms holding you?
You are always in My arms, you are always in My heart...
With your eyes I contour the stars and I offer you the
world,
All I do is for you,
All there exists is My gift for you.

My beloved...
My love... I exist for you...

Upon receiving this answer my heart transformed into a prayer:

Please, Lord, keep this declaration alive in me... Allow me to always live through You and never through myself... You be me, because I don't need to be me anymore... Be You in all that my mind, my thought, my hand, my soul sets upon...

Be You and through me, You do everything!

JOURNAL

*T*here was a theatre festival in town and I had offered lodging to some of the artists. As a result, I did some housework: cleaning, painting the doors, washing, general cleaning as you might say. I was really enthusiastic about meeting them so I prepared everything with great love. But, all of a sudden, something in me cried:

Oh, Lord, I think that I'll only have time to finish the book if you put me to bed.

It had been such a long time since I had written any pages for the book.

I was always finding something else to do.Actually, there are always many things to do. So, in order to realise something, you must stay focused.

I continued with the cleaning, thinking that in a week the festival would be over and then I would organise myself better, making time to write too.

I had put the first layer of paint on two doors and then I had to paint them again the next day. I also started to wash a mattress and put it in the bathtub with water and detergent.

That was yesterday.

Enthused to continue my work, I woke up early this morning. I decided I had to wash the mattress first in order to clear the bathroom so I could clean it then. The door painting wouldfollow and so on. When I decided to remove the mattress from the bathtub I realised that it was very heavy from all the water. There was no way to drain it; I had to leave it on the margin of the bathtub.

As I tried to straighten my back whilst lifting the mattress, I felt a terrible pain in the middle of my back. I stopped, stood for a whileand then I continued with my work, in spite of all the pain. The mattress was finally on the side of the bathtub, but my back was stuck and in great pain.

In my thoughtless enthusiasm, I had hurt my back in such a way that I could no longer move.

There was no way I could continue with the preparations.

I was in great pain and I could barely get into bed; I was finding it difficult to get into a comfortable position.

With regret I had to tell the organisers that I couldn't help them anymore. As a therapist, I knew that in the best-case scenario you could recover from such a condition in about two months.

As I was in bed, I had the chance to reflect and I realised that I had received what I had asked for: yesterday I had said I'll continue to write only if I have to stay in bed and now I was in bed.

I understood what had been the cause of my problem and now, all I could do was to make a deal with God.

I asked Him: **Lord, will you cure me if I promise I'll write every day for fourhours?**

I felt that if I prayed, I'd have the chance to be miraculously healed.

So, I mentally prepared myself to write the book. I was unable to start writing on the first day because it was difficult to find a comfortable position. I didn't know how to position myself in a waythat the suffering I was feeling (because of all the pain) would not get transmitted into my writing.

My aim was that the readers of this book should be able to feel God's grace and love. But in a state of suffering, I knew the words would be impregnated with that pain and that was what the reader would receive.

After a day, I got used to the pain and the suffering reduced. I was feeling at ease and happy in my soul so I did as I had promised: I started to write.

WHEN WE FORGET, HE REMINDS US

Yes, sometimes we forget. Human nature has its attachments, needs and inert desires.

I had already been beyond the threshold for a long time. God was the centre of my attention. My life was in almost perfect harmony. At least that was what I thought then. Later I understood that the learning process and all its experiences never end.

My relationship with God was as great as it could have been. I knew that if I asked, I would receive, be it a physical thing or just an answer.

Each problem had a solution, all questions had an answer. All that was left unresolved was a piece of land we had not been able to sell for a few years.

Selling it was a necessity for us. We wanted to use the money to repay a bank loan we had taken in order to construct another building in the mountain, next to our guesthouse.

One day, God told me:

Spend one hour with Me each morning and another one each evening. Don't ask for anything else and you'll see what happens.

- *Alright Lord, that's what I'll do.*

I relaxed and I left everything in His care. I hadn't asked for anything else for myself or for others. Each morning and evening, I would do my hour of meditation with Him. During the rest of the day, I followed my daily routine.

Here is what happened:

Day 1:

- I started my *tapas*.

Day 2:

- At first, a state of relaxation appeared. I hadn't even noticed how tense I had become. We believe that we always have to do something, but that's not the case.

  With all the projects in my life, my sleep had been disturbed duringthe last few months. More than that, I used to feel that if I slept, I would be wasting time that I could use to sort out other things. Dark circles appeared around my eyes and I always felt that I never had enough time in the day.

  Because God had told me not to ask for anything, I was not in a hurry anymore. I'd forgotten how it was to relax. I didn't only have a good night's sleep, but I was also able to have afternoon naps, which was fabulous. All of a sudden there was no pressure. I was simply existing.

  Oh, how good it is when nothing is bothering you and you trust that God does everything for you!

- On the evening of the same day, God revealed to me a very powerful method to access the causal body and to be able to either materialise soothing or to erase karma, depending on how you wished to use it.

  I will teach that method in the second module of the Happiness Course.

Day 3:

- I received a surprise gift – I went to see my dentist. I had known her for a long time and she has a certain sympathy for me. Today, she surprised me: she had everything she needed for a whitening treatment and she was going to start it the same day. I was very surprised. I had wanted that treatment for a while, it's true, but I never had the money to invest in it. All our funds were goingtowards the construction of the new building.

- Someone else also gave me an unexpected gift: three natural pearl necklaces and a bracelet.

Why was I so impressed with the pearls? Let me tell you the story:

Long ago, we were snorkelling in the Red Sea. As we swam over the corals, I saw an opened oyster and in it there was a pearl. It was so fascinating to see it in its natural environment. I picked up the oyster with the pearl in it. I wanted to bring it home, as a memory. As I got back on the boat, the diving instructor saw the oyster; he took it and returned it to the sea. It seemed a fair gesture. What would happen if every diver vandalised the sea, claiming they were entitled to take souvenirs? But in my soul, there remained a small amount of regret. And this is how such a small attachment cancreatekarma.

After a few years, we visited Puri, one of the holy cities of India. This place has a special story, but I'll tell that story some other time. Here is how a God-loving soul is rewarded by Him who is Love itself. As I was walking on the beach, someone approached me and offered me tennatural pearls for a very small price. Of course, I took them because I was still attached to the lost pearl. I was so happy and it was as though I held the greatest fortune in my hand. It's fascinating how these small pearls are created.

Back in Romania, after I finished the Happiness Course with a new series, I offered a pearl to each of the graduates. I wanted to offer them something special and the pearl was part of my gift tothem. To me, the pearl was a real jewel, especially because it came from that sacred place and thus it had a special spiritual relevance. I offered them the pearls happily, without regret. Now they multiplied in this gift, as though my love had had that effect on them.

God takes care of our karma too, if we leave ourselves to His Will. What do we have to do? We have to abandon ourselves to Him, completely trusting Him. This is how my attachment to a pearl created the karma that God consumed for me during the time he asked me to be with Him and trust Him.

Day 4:

This day brought an observation, an awareness about the Happiness Course. My eyes were being opened: it was best to do as God suggested - one class each week and not as a camp. In a camp, the state of communion with God would appear at the end, the end being such a short time that a strong base couldn't be built.

I thanked God for this awareness.

Day 5:

- We signed a contract that would bring us about one thousand euros,
- The evening meditation was a lesson, a beautiful lesson from God. At somepoint, as I was deepening in my heart, I felt how I was ascending from the *heart void,* through the *median void* to the *supreme void* and stepping into transcendence, or as otherwise said, entering the Kingdom of God.

    That was today's most precious gift.
- Another valuable gift was receiving land, as a present, worth ten to twelve thousand euros.
- Another lesson that I've learnt is that by entering into this sacred space of the heart during meditation, and having that state of communion with God, is that any sickness can be cured. This is the best medicine for everything.

    I speak from personal experience – all day, that day, I had been bothered by ear pain till the evening meditation when, feeling God's presence in my heart, the pain disappeared never to return.
- My faith was tested today: all the funds that we had available were gone and till the next week there was no possibility, as far as I knew, to receive any other money. So, having promised I won't ask, I haven't.

    Nothing was lacking; we had enough to eat and today we received two more bags of food so that our immediate future needs were also satisfied. It was just the idea of not having any money, in case we might need it.

I trusted God completely and, as I promised, I didn't ask.

My daily meditations were bringing me to a state of detachment from the world.

Day 6:

- I felt an impulse to start a new series of the Happiness Course. Now is the moment. It was always God who was to choose the moment, not me. I do nothing in that direction until He gives me clear signs that I must do it again.

  I still have no money and I am not asking either.

Day 7:

- We signed a contract that would bring us one thousand euros in fourdays.

Day 8:

- This was the day when I receive patients for therapy. But today, one after the other, they excused themselves for not being able to pay me today and asked me to wait till next week. I knew it was a new test.

  I promised I wouldn't ask so I didn't.
- We signed another contract, this time bringing us two thousand euros in twomonths.

Day 9:

- A very beautiful and powerful method of forgiveness was revealed to me by God
- A new contract was signed, bringing us five hundredeuros.

Day 10:

- What a surprise, God! There is a buyer for that land! That land we were trying to sell for years! This is a real surprise!
- Another surprise: my dentist said she'd do all the work for free. Even though I told her that I have the money to pay for it, she said she wanted to give it to me as a gift.

Day 11:

God, what are you doing? I received two thousand euros as a gift. I'm completely amazed.

Day 12:

- During my evening meditation, God told me that the heart, where I meet Him, is the source of all knowledge.
  Thank You Lord!

Day 13:

Today God resolved a love-related situation that seemed impossible to get out of. It's amazing! It's like the angels tied what was untied and brought to light what had been in darkness.

Day 14:

Today is Mahashivaratri

A very special spiritual field was manifested on this night. I meditated till midnight and then I fell asleep for tenminutes. My Kundalini energy awakened and all my bodies vibrated. In the astral realm, a Kundalini awakening is perceived differently, in a more complete and conscious way. I experienced ecstasy.

It was a remarkable experience and now, for the first time, I understood why they say that on this night, Shiva bestows His Grace upon human beings. Next year I'll pay more attention and I'll meditate more onMahashivaratri.

Day 15:

I was inspired by God to organise a workshop with the graduates of the Happiness Course on March 28th and 29th. He even told me what to do on that occasion.

I felt that this meeting was prepared somewhere in Heaven, and it wouldbe a very special moment.

Full of joy, I started to announce the event to the students.

Day 16:

I received two thousand euros as a gift.

Day 17:

I won one thousand euros.

Day 18:

God exemplified to me the state of perfect detachment. I felt this state would lead me to the state of purity I've always dreamed of.

Day 19:

Today I raised my voiceas I was scolding someone who had made some mistakes. A while after I left, I felt guilty, thinking I shouldn't have been so harsh. I felt I could have been gentler.

I couldn't wait to start my evening meditation so I could ask God's forgiveness.

But in the evening, barely had I started my meditation and, the answer echoed in my heart. Sometimes we need to be like that, harsh and firm with certain people who are complacent in ignorance. I then felt a great compassion for them and a great love from God. There was nothing to forgive because He wasn't upset with me about what I had done.

Oh, Lord, how wrongly do we understand these things! How could God ever be upset?

Day 20:

This morning we sold the land for 31,500 euros. Contrary to our expectations, we were very detached fromthis action, doing it as though it was for somebody else and not for us.

Day 21:

I started to work today on a conference about Kedarnath. It is part of a series of conferences about India that I am delivering. When I started on the subject of the Pandavas, trying to explain their symbol, my heart chakra (Anahata Chakra) was activated so powerfully that I could barely control my body.

I felt God transmitting knowledge through me, as a symbol of the Mahabharata. Thank You Lord! I am profoundly grateful to You.

(I've written about Kedarnath and the Pandavas in a previous chapter.)

Day 22:

I received an important lesson during my morning meditation.

God told me *that I can have a completely pure mind if I can remain totally focused on His Being and also if I don't ask or pray for anything.*

Any type of attachment pollutes the mind and distances us from God.

Then He told me how I couldreally have a perfectly pure mind.

I also felt that having a pure mind is absolutely essential to attain liberation.

Day 23:

I received another important message today: *by having access to the causal plane, you can instantly know the cause of everything happening not only with you but also with all that is around you, even other people around you.*

Day 24:

- I started a new series of the Happiness Course. It was much easier than my earlier courses to get people to subscribe.

  I lived fully the emotion of starting this new course and the emotion of God, waiting for this meeting with them.
- Today the Annunciation is celebrated and we also received some unexpected news. There is a buyer for the land that was given to us. Yet again, God doesn't bother about money and gave us this good news when others think that the Annunciation is onlyabout fasting and ascesis.

Day 25:

With the money I received as a gift, I bought a car today. This morning I felt that my car was waiting for me. I didn't have to search toomuch for it. Guided by the Angels I went to exactly where it was. It was a quick and efficient transaction.

Day 26:

Today is the first day of my workshop on happiness. There were tenin the group - the ninewho attended, plus me. The exact size that God said a class must be. The first day went really well. We had His support and there was a lot of Grace. God made us feel His presence. He awakened a great joy in our hearts and offered us wonderful experiences.

Day 27:

Two weeks ago, God told me that Heaven's gates will open with the occasion of this workshop. I was curiously waiting to see what would happen... I was thinking about my students, especially some of them, the more advanced ones, and how they wouldreceive the (spiritual) gifts offered to them during this meeting. This moment had beenprepared since yesterday. The outpouring of Grace continued till the last moment, the climax.

The heavens opened during the final meditation. I became One with Everything and I truly understood what God means.

I understood my situation. Once beyond the threshold, you are one with God and you are consciously creating the universes and the experiences that you wish to live. You are no longer simply subjected to the cause and effect. I understood this creation of our minds, a creation that can be reabsorbed in any minute because it doesn't exist longer than we wish it to exist.

Only now did I realise what it means to be one with God.

Once you are one with God there is no longer that separation. You are not one with God, you are God. You are Him, the One. I felt that for the first time in my life. So, as He said, the Heavens opened.

During the meditation, I was not feeling that I am with God but I felt, and since then I feel this continuously, that I AM, I am the One.

This is indeed a new level and I know that from now on, this is how I'll do my meditations...not with God...but with I am.

The students also had special experiences. The Heavens opened for them too.

Some of them felt God, heard His voice or saw His Light. Others experienced other uniquestates.

I realised another important aspect. That the Bodhisattvas are the ones who understood what God is. How can you liberate yourself? What an illusion for the liberated ones to believe that they are liberated! How can you liberate yourself and a great number of people whostill struggle in ignorance? We are ONE, we are truly liberated when all of us are liberated. And by making an effort to help others reach this state, you are also helping yourself.

I also understood the saying: God is experimenting Himself in His creation.

Day 28:

I felt some things today. I'm starting to see and understand the world from a different perspective, that of Oneness.

At first, yesterday, I felt I am love. As I was thinking about the love that God gives, the love we give Him, the love for other people, I felt that by loving, I am loving myself. I can't differentiate between love, the loved one and me, the one who loves…so…I am love.

Then today, I felt I am Happiness and that I am all there is because I am one with everything.

Till now I could only understand mentally the statement that the act of meditation, the one who meditates and the object of meditation are one. Now I am living it. It is so interesting.

I feel my evolution is on another level and I am still taking steps forward; new amazing experiences await me.

Even the meditation that God asked me to do is now different. I cannot say I that I go deep into my heart to meet Him because He is everywhere around me now.

The meditation became I AM, a feeling of simply **being**.

I feel these are just the first steps. It is interesting. Very interesting. A new world opened up for me.

Today, as I was teaching about the act of consecration (giving to the Divine all the fruits of our actions), I understood it from this perspective. We perform the consecration in order not to create new karma, so that we don't generate causes that will produce effects. The effects are now very evident because, as I am one with everything, all I am doing, I'm doing it to myself. This is the secret. All the actions are upon me - this is the secret of the fruits of our actions. Like I would deliberately hit my hand and then I would be surprised that it is hurting me.

As they say:*What you give is what you get.*This statement is as real as possible. Now, feeling that I am one with everything, it is clear to me that each action I do, I actually do it for myself.

It is so interesting

I feel like I entered into a new universe that I'm now beginning to explore.

What You have offered me now, my Lord, is such a big Grace.

What *You* have offered me?

What I have offered to myself.

It's really interesting what is happening now.

Day 29:
- **The realisations are continuing. It's amazing!**

Today I bought some meat for my dogs and as I was walking with it in my bag, I asked myself if this is a spiritual thing - accepting that other animals are killed so I can feed my dogs. I instantly realised that I, that meat and all the animals (both the one that was slayed and my dogs) are one. Then who is killing who? Who is eating who? It's just a form of energy transfer from one part to the other in this great Whole.

Then my question was - how will I meditate now - because I cannot say anymore that I'll go deepinto my heart and find God there. I really feel that when I made the leap, the heart's void filled itself and poured out. Now, if I try to get in, there is no void, there is just Gods plenitude overflowing.

So I thought I'll meditate on I AM.

In the evening I realised that actually, when I meditate, the meditation's object and the meditation are always one. This always happens and this is how I should continue my practice, by being one with the meditation and the meditation's object.

All I have to do now is to think of the idea of meditation and instantly, all three unite, no matter the theme that I choose. It's an instant union as soon as the idea of meditation appears.

- Meanwhile I was enjoying new experiences of Oneness. As I sat on the terrace, I heard a bird singing. It caught my attention and that made me become one with it. I felt its states, its concerns, its emotions.
- It happened with everything: wherever I directed my attention or my eyes, I became One with that thing.
- I received information about what to teach on the second module of this course whichwill be named:

The happiness of the communion with God

Day 30:

Becoming one with the meditation and the meditation's object became a constant. It's funny that I can't meditate on God anymore because He is no longer outside me and there is no place where I can direct my attention to. I am God and in order to meditate on Him, I should get outside of me and I can't do that. I am inside and outside, I am everywhere.

Conclusion

By doing what God had asked me to do, money started to come my way, as if it was sent from the sky. I didn't have any social problems or health issues or difficultiesof any other kind,and my spiritual state ascended tounexpected levels.

All in one month. A month when I spent an hour with God every morning and another hour every evening. I completely abandoned myself to Him. I hadn't asked for anything, I hadn'tprayed any more, trusting that God knows what's best, He knows what I need and He will give me that.

Indeed, since my eyes were opened and I stepped onto thespiritual path, it was a difficult road with many struggles and tests. I even had outbursts with people and some might say: *Who, she? This woman met God? She had spiritual states?! Impossible!*

We all have a life to live and we live it as we know best.

I know that I started from zero and I craved so much to know God until I did.

I know that it was Him who kept me in His hands and under His caring and loving guidance, He led me to Himself.

He is our supreme master, teacher, guru or whatever you want to call Him.

He is the most direct way to Himself.

Part III

SOME TEACHINGS

I haven't invented these teachings. On my way towards Him, God inspired me and often talked to me. The teachings that follow are His teachings.

I cannot say they have an order or that one is more important than the other. So even though you will find them put down in a particular order, from my point of view, they are all equally important.

JOURNAL

*T*oday is the celebration of the Archangels Michael and Gabriel. I started the day with a state of joy in my soul and also with a lot of love for God.

I said Happy Anniversary to all my friends with names derived from Michael and Gabriel and then I continued writing about the teachings:

1. God loves us very much. He loves us equally, without showing any difference.

We rejoice-oh, the stereotypical language! That's what we should do, rejoice. But many do not because they don't know this truth.

I'll say it again: we have God's love from the moment we were created. For different reasons (education, religion, the society we live in, ignorance or simply forgetting, etc) many of us don't acknowledge the existence of this love and others, who discovered that God loves us, believe they are not amongst the lucky ones.

Many think that they don't deserve His love or, because they cannot feel Him, they cannot imagine that His love exists.

Others think they are sinners and that God loves only the pious ones, the devoted ones.

Others say that God loves the ones who are rich, who have luck in love matters, who are healthy, successful. As for them - the poor ones, without any chance of thriving, not loved by anyone - they are not loved by God.

Totally wrong!

God loves everyone equally. The poor and the rich, the ill and the healthy, the pious and the sinner, the successful and the unsuccessful.

It is just our minds that create differences not God.

We live in duality, we perceive the world as duality. In order to recognise something, we need the opposite: white - black, night - day, bad – good, hot – cold, etc. God is beyond duality. Those who think that God is vengeful, punishing, judgmental, angry, inflicting suffering...those people are very wrong.

God is joy, love, infinite understanding and forgiveness. He never judges and is overwhelming in His kindness.

Being beyond duality, He doesn't differentiate amongst people.

All human beings are equally endowed with the Divine Light.

God doesn't judge and give more to some and less to others; all have the same chance forliberation, to return home, in His arms.Otherwise, how would you explain all the situations when the ones wandering, the criminals, the lost ones, managed in a moment to become illuminated and instantly transform themselves?

We are all equal in God's eyesand He loves us the same, no matter who we are or what we have done. Only we, humans, think that some of us deserve more love than others. God doesn't think like that.

The thought of being loved by someone is so reassuring and, knowing that we are loved by God, brings so much peace into our souls.

So I ask you now, live with joy in your souls because God loves you, He loves you so much, so deeply, more than any lover would.

If you open your heart to feel His love, your entire life will change. By living with love in your soul you will have more trust. By having more trust, you will be successful in all that you do, you will have the courage to operate in every work field, in every situation because you know for sure that He, who created everything, loves you very much.

I'm saying it again, even if I'm repeating myself: have trust, God loves you!

Enjoy His love, open up your heart and let it fill you.

JOURNAL

I felt the need to take a break from writing. Sitting on the chair is uncomfortable and painful, so I needed a break to lie on the bed and relax.

I turned on the TV and clicked on a random channel; it was showing a movie about angels and their mission on earth. It was towards the middle of the film and I wasn't able to understand the action but I persevered because I liked the idea. I didn't learn anything about the plot till the end. I just saw those angels fulfilling their missions. I loved the idea.

Then the film ended.

My husband brought me my meal in bed. Because my back was still stiff and in great pain, it would've been difficult for me to go into the kitchen and eat my meal there.

At some point, I don't know precisely what happened, but I felt something on my right side. It was like someone, maybe an Angel or even God Himself, was offering me the chance to choose my healing. I was the one to choose if I would heal or not. Of course, my soul said **yes.** *My soul, not I. My soul, not my ego. It was like a zero point, a hiatus, a turning point where you could make any choice. It was the moment for a miracle: the next minute I was healed. I was amazed. Is something like this even possible? I couldn't believe it… Was I really healed?*

Perplexed, I uttered to my husband:

- **I think I am healed.**

As he was eating, he looked at me and couldn't believe it. I bent to the front and I was able to touch my toes with my hands and even place my head on my knees. Could I really do it?

- Stay, don't force it, he told me.
- He'd had a hernia and he knew how it was.
- But look, I can do it! I said happily to him.
- Your mobility is better than mine, he said with amazement.

It was a total wonder. I went to the bathroom, I bent over the bathtub and I felt myself light as a feather – there was no blockage, no tension.

As he looked at me with amazement, jokingly he said:

\- Send me the angel who cured you!

The promise I made to God healed me and now I had to keep it. I could not stop until I finished the book. I must write daily, at least for four hours a day.

So, I continued to write.

2. He offers us all we wish for.

All we need to do is to wish for it or to accept what He is offering, even though we may not have asked for it.

In other words, God is fulfilling all of our wishes.

There is a great blockage in the human mind regarding this Truth.

If God loves us so deeply, what reasons would He have not to offer us what we wish for?

A parent would do anything for their child and, as per their capabilities, they would offer him all that he wished for.

God is more than a parent for us and He has infinite possibilities. So if I, a human from this world, want something, why wouldn't He give it to me? What would be His reasons?

God is not sadistic to keep telling you -*I won't give that to you* -if He sees us wishing for something.

God is not judging so He will never say:*You don't deserve it.*

Our mind is the only thing that judges and thinks that God doesn't want to give us what we are asking for. We are so unjust to God by believing that.

Jesus said: *Ask and you shall receive.*

Whenever He promises, He will keep that promiseforever. He won't change His mind, He won't goback on his word, He won't turn His back on us, and He won't abandon us.

We, humans, are doing all those things, not God.

Jesus was God's voice on earth and through Him, many truths have been transmitted to us. So if God said -*Ask and you shall receive* - then so it will be.

Jesus didn't say – wait, we have to see if you deserve it, if you prayed enough, if you've been good. He only said: *Whenever you are praying, do it in such a way as though you have already received what you are asking for.* So there is no if, there is no doubt, no hesitation, in believing that God will give us what we are asking for.

I am talking now about what we desire and not what we need.

Many believe that God gives us only what we need. They believe that He is so good and watchful that He will give us what we need to exist, to move on, to survive, to get out of the trouble we're in.

Our minds are saying that and not God. Our minds are putting limits to all that we receive, to all that we need.

God is giving us much more.

God gives us all we are asking for.

Any wish that might cross our minds, even if it is for just a second, is put on His list and, at the right time, it will come to us.

When is the right time?

Whenever we let it be, whenever we choose it.

It crosses our minds that we would like a palace. God will put that wish on the list and then the mind comes and says: *Oh my, how can I have a palace when I am so poor? With my small salary, I would need at least tenlives to save the money for a palace. How would I take care of it? To clean so many rooms? And the bills?* And so on…These negative and pessimistic thoughts that arise put a distance between us and the moment the palace will be ours.

But if we would do as Jesus said, to ask as though we had already received it, with all ourfaith in the promise that God made to us when He said: *Ask and you shall receive,* then the palace will soon be ours.

We don't need to think of a thing as being small or big, or that we deserve it or not, or even if it's right for us or not. If we wish for it, we will receive it because God keeps His promises.

It doesn't matter if we ask for small things or great things. They might seem small or big to us because we live in duality but to God, asking for a packet ofmatches or a palace is the same thing.

We will receive what we are asking for and God will give it to us with infinite joy.

Don't put limits to your requests.

Don't think that it is spiritual to live without things.

Being One with God means having access to His entire creation.

God is plenitude and He hasn't asked us to live in poverty.

He offered us the whole world with all His love.

Ask! Ask with trust, with faith, because you deserve it. You deserve to live in abundance, to have beautiful things and all that you are dreaming of.

It's a contradiction seeing beings that claim to have attained a certain spiritual level and yet they are struggling with poverty, helplessness, hunger and illness.

The closer you are to God, the better you will see the gates of the Kingdom of Heaven opening to you. There resides plenitude and abundance.

It is totally different if an ascetic, who has attained a high spiritual level, has chosen penitence and fasting. It is his choice and he lives the wayhe has chosen to. But when you say you are one with God and you suffer hunger (and I say suffer), it means a sense of lacking and separation from God.

A man who consciously chooses penitence and asceticism is not suffering. That is the paradise he has chosen and he is happy. When you are one with God, you are happy. An ascetic is not lying when he or she says they are on the path to God. They need nothing from this world unlike others who are sick, overwrought, lonely and so on.

From this point of view, I want to point out the wrong vision that Christians have of Jesus.

Whenever you see a Christian symbol you see the cross and most often, Jesus in pain, covered in blood, dead.

People, this is not Jesus!

I am saying it using the present tense because Jesus was not, Jesus IS.

He left but He returned as promised. He didn't leave us. He came here for the second time. He is here, in our hearts, in the hearts of all those who have received Him.

A Being who brought God's Word on earth is not thin, defeated or dead. Why then, do Christians picture Him like that?

Whoever felt or sees our dear Lord Jesus will know that he is full of strength, energy and courage, He is ravishingly beautiful (because the outside is a reflection of the inside and He who isperfect is most certainly perfectly beautiful).

Only a few artists sensed Him the way He really is and depicted Him full of power and energy.

The Christian symbol is the Resurrection. Because of this Resurrection we believe in Jesus. So why are we depicting Him on the cross, tormented and dead instead of representing Him alive, resurrected, full of light and energy?

That is the light and the life of Christianity.

It is only this human belief of deserving the lacking, the sufferance, the sickness and death that prevents us from daring to believe that we deserve more.

Yes, good people, you deserve all that is good in this world because you are one with God, you are everything, so you have access to everything.

Dare to believe and to ask!

The Hindu culture represents Lord Shiva (God) as a man with beautiful traits, muscular, dressed as an ascetic, showing us that asceticism is a part of plenitude also. He has access to everything, He knows everything and He has a great love for His devotees. He also shows us that every being, be it an animal, a human, a god or a demon, will receive what they are asking for through prayers.

I won't compare, analyse or point out the differences among religions. I believe there is only one God who is everywhere; He is unique and His paths are infinite.

I remember also the advice that God gave to His believers - not to try to represent Him in a way. Yes, He was right, so right

because we don't know how He looks and any representation would not contain all of its reality.

But why have I remembered the Hindu representation? It was to point out that some sensed it and wished to transmit that to the believers: God is plenitude, beauty, abundance and He is fulfilling all our prayers.

Anyone has easily access to God if they love Him, say the Hindu legends.

It doesn't matter which name you use for God as long as you see Him as who He is.

The Bible said that God made man in His resemblance.

What will I see when I look in the mirror then? It is God and more than that.

Jesus said: *The Father and I are one but He is more than Me.*

By seeing myself in the mirror, I see God. But I can't see Him as whole, as He really is, it's just a part of Him.

So why do Christians depict Him with a thin and tormented face? Am I the same? Do I want to be the same? Is this the resemblance of God, His plenitude and perfection?

The most beautiful representation of Jesus that I ever saw was on a beach in Madurai, India. I bought it.

As I write now, I am looking into His eyes, at that beautiful representation, and I feel that this is the closest image(as much as can be transmitted through a painting) to who He really is.

The idea of this subchapter is that of Wholeness, because God comes towards us with everything.

Open up your hearts and receive what He is offering.

3. God is not separated from us.

Many people believe that we live in total separation from God. But He is not separate from us. He is waiting for us to return. All those stories of Jesus knocking at our door are true, even though we have heard them so many times and they bore usnow. With simple words, God transmits many messages to us. If we'd apply those, we'd be forever happy. We've heard them so many times now and they are flat; they seem like simple stories or we believe we already know these things.

I am sorry for my words. I too was one of those voices like so many people, saying that the story of Jesus knocking at our door is a naive one.

All of them have an inaccurate understanding of the Truth.

God never was, He is not and He never will be separated from us. He is in us, He is with us. He acts through us and He lives through us.

Is it our mind that is separating us from God? No, the mind is not so powerful that it canseparate us from God. The mind is just creating the illusion of separation. It creates the illusion that God is somewhere further away, in an inaccessible Heaven and, in order to reach Him, we need to make great efforts which,however, are not a guarantee for us to reach Him.

God is not so distant, God is not distant at all. He is right here, next to you, in you, in all that you are and in all that exists.

Why would we then look for Him in a distant Heaven that is difficult to reach?

When did this false affirmation appear? Who said it so confidently that all humanity started to believe it?

If God is all there is, how could we believe that there will be another place, without God, where we are? So that we'd then have to make efforts, full of faith, aspiration and devotion to reach the Kingdom of God, or Heaven, where He lives…

All those who found God have found Him in their hearts. If He is not there, then He is nowhere. Once we find Him there, many secrets and mysteries will be revealed to us.

So I return to the main idea: we are separated from God by our own lack of knowledge. This allegory of Jesus standing in front of our door, waiting for us to open it is a way of expressing the fact that He is There and it's up to us to see Him.

4. If we want to know the Ultimate Divine Truth, then the first step is to speak and live in the spirit of Truth.

Most people have a mask for each of life's situations and consider that this is the right thing: at home you are one person, you are another person at work, another one in society, someone else in a certain environment and so on. People consider this the only way to deal with this world.

But all these masks are distancing us from who we really are.

If we knew who we are, maybe it wouldn't be so bad, but it still isn't fair from a divine point of view.

If we do not know who we are and frequently hide behind masks, what then are the opportunities to find out who we really are?

Many people identify themselves with their masks and they are completely lost if they lose the chance to use them. People are grasping onto something that is not real and they believe it is the truth in their life.

Only by gradually coming out from behind the masks, because it would be too difficult to do it at once, do we get the chance to find out at a certain time the Truth about ourselves. These masks are mere lies, distancing us from God.

When Moses asked the burning bush that was speaking to him to tell him who it is, the answer was: *I am That I Am.*

Then we, who desire to reach God, who wish to know the truth, if we know we were created in His resemblance, why would we want to be anyone else other than **who we are?**

If I am like this, why would I appear otherwise in different places?

To seem better, more serious, more peaceful, more responsible…more…more…more…when I am not like that at all… Why? Just to impress someone? And then, when I am alone with myself I become depressed because I don't know who I am? Each mask is related to the place and society it is used for. When we are alone, we hang our masks in the closet and, whenwe look in the mirror, we are scared of seeing a head without a face. Yes, it's an expression, a way of pronouncingthat none of those masks relate to who we really are and there are moments when we remain without them. In those moments, we are lost.

We cannot play with the Truth of our life, with the Truth of our existence.

Our lives are a theatre, reincarnation over reincarnation, until someone shouts: *And who am I really?*

I lived as a woman, as a man, as a rich man or as a beggar, a simple man or a monk, a businessman or a missionary. Each time, when the moment of death came, I left my mask behind and I went. I'm leaving mask after mask, life after life. I use mask after mask in a single life and I lose myself amongst them, not knowing who I am.

The first simple step, a common sense one too, in establishing the Truth about ourselves, is to let go of all the masks.

To be who we are, as God is: *I am That I Am.*

By using so many masks we forget who we really are!

By giving up on the masks we come closer to our own soul.

The more we delve into ourselves, the more we will be able to see that there are masks we use even for ourselves. We believe ourselves to be someone other than who we really are. This is the mind's game. I believe I am a genius but in fact I am big fool. I believe I am spiritual but I am really ignorant.

I believe everybody respects and loves me and actually the people are polite to me out of interest or fear.

There can be also positive examples: a beautiful woman believing she is ugly, a talented man believing he has no gifts and so on.

The illusion about ourselves is very big and most of the time, we have wrong impressions.

For sure, we'd all want to know who we really are and who we truly are.

Any soul gets tired after so many moments of wandering.

By having a sincere wish and a lot of common sense, gradually we'll be able to cancel that false image of ourselves and be able to quit our masks.

Only then will we be able to appear without a mask in our relationship with God and only then can we start getting closer, truly closer to Him.

What does it mean to have masks in your relationship with God?

It is to believe that you are in communion with Him, and yet be nervous, agitated, always upset, ill, lacking empathy, betraying others and just following your own interests.

It's easy to understand that God is not like that and as long as you are in communion with Him, you cannot be like thateither.

I usually say that he who has experienced *Samadhi* is transformed; he is not the same anymore. It is enough to know perfection once; then you cannot behave in the same way again. You will be different. Things will naturally transform in your being and they will bring you closer to perfection.

When we are able to appear without masks in front of God, then we are on the direct path towards knowing the Truth.

We know that we cannot hide from the face of God. We know he sees us, He knows all we are doing, all we are thinking, even our intentions.

Then who are we trying to fool?

Ourselves.

We are fooling ourselves, we are fooling one another and thus we are lightyears away from the Truth.

The good news is that these lightyears can be reduced to just one moment, the present moment, where we truly desire to be who we really are.

That's why it is true to say that even in the last moment of life you can return to God. Even that counts.

It's all our choice, to give up on being the actor and just manifesting our Divine simplicity.

This is the recipe for reducing those lightyears away from the Truth to a moment. The moment is our choice.

And thus, returning to the subject: who are we actually? How will we get to live the truth about our beings?

By starting to recognise the truth in our life, in all the situations that arise. We speak only the truth and we live in the spirit of truth.

Did you know that if we respect the truth completely (100%), after about a month we'll become prophets? Oh, relax, don't be scared! It's not a desecration. It's mathematics.

Let me explain: by only saying the truth we'll enter into such a resonance with the Divine Truth that we won't be able to utter even the smallest lie, even by mistake.

Let me give you an example: if for a month you strictly respect the truth, day after day, then, after a month if you thought of saying that ten people will enter your house in the evening that will be so. All that you say will happen for sure because all you have said till then was true. You're already in an aura of truth where nothing is false. In this aura, you have a great chance of discovering the Truth about yourself.

You might say: *Yes, but a prophet is more than a man who speaks the truth.*

Do you think it is so easy to speak and live in the name of the Truth?

It's not that easy. Only an honest, pure and righteous being would be able to do it. Those people who have been known as prophets were actually guardians of the truth. They were so correct, honest and spoke with so much common sense that they never allowed themselves to lie or to cheat on someone, not even on themselves or God.

By following the Truth in your life, you will find the truth about yourself and that will help you attain a real communion with God. By being in communion with Him, you'll know the Truth that only He knows.

Each untruth is distancing us from the Divine Truth and thus we are programming other new lives in illusion.

Parents, for example, tell many lies to their children in order to get them to eat, to go to bed or to do what they want them to do.

Yes, it might seem then that we are getting what we are wishing for but, in fact, each of those lies is distancing us from God.

God is Truth and by not saying the truth we are moving away from Him.

The path to God is an easy one but we are complicating it because of the image we have of ourselves and how we want others to see us.

The moment when loneliness brings us so much joy because we are finally alone with ourselves, it is then that we start to express the truth through our words and our deeds.

Then loneliness is not frightening anymore. It becomes a blessing.

The Truth is very important in our relationship with God;

You can create false relationships with people, but not with God.

You can tell others things that are not true in order to maintain your relationship with them and they won't know the truth because they are not in resonance with it, but you cannot build a relationship with God on something that is false. It's impossible.

With every lie, we deepen into a life of illusion. With every truth we speak,we are getting closer to the Divine Truth.

I am not calling you liars; please forgive me if that's what you think. Because of the many untruthful things we have said during our past lives and this one, we have delved more and more into the illusion so that now, we cannot distinguish between what is true in our lives and what is not.

It's about time to end this fantasy and have a real life.

What does it mean to live in the spirit of Truth?

It means to listen to our soul.

How many times have we done things our soul didn't want us to do? How many times did we listen to others even if our soul wanted something else?

So we should ask ourselves: how many times have we lied to our soul by saying or doing things other than what we wanted to? You want to say that you had no choice, that this is the life you live, the family you are a part of, the job you have, etc...

We are exactly where we choose to be.

We have created our own illusion in which we live, no matter whether we know it or not, or if we like it or not.

The good news it's that it is not eternal. We can change it right now, by creating a new reality based on the truth.

If we have the courage to recognise that we don't like things that we have kept doing for years, from now on we simply don't need to do it. In this way, we won't be lying to ourselves or to the others involved and our life will be simpler.

One by one, we should take the situations in our lives and create order in them. To end all compromises and do what our soul desires.

You'll say that it is not that easy but I amtelling you that it is very easy. It's all up to you – to believe, to wish it, to decide and to take action.

Be brave and step out of this illusory life you live in.

You don't need to offend others by telling them the truth totheir faces, but if this truth is important in your life, speakit or simply act according to it.

Here is a simple example: every Sunday we go to our parents' place and have lunch with them. We don't like to do soall the time. Sometimes we do enjoyit, but not every Sunday. It became an obligation and now we don't know how to stop it without offending them. So what do we do? We will simply choose not to go there. Instead of going and putting a mask on, pretending fake good moods and not being ourselves, we'd be better off staying at home, going for a walk or doing anything else that our soul seeks to do.

We'll let our parent know that we're not going and if we are asked why, then we won't invent an excuse but we'll say the truth: *Today I feel like staying at home* or*Today I want to go to the cinema or for a walk.*

Maybe they will get upset but, you know, every emotionlasts for three days. They will get over it and you will be happy that you have listened to your soul.

Any compromise moves us away from the soul. As we become distant, we also become cold and robotic, and our emotions and feelings are frozen. Illnesses will appear over time and even an early death because the soul cannot resist frustration for so long.

The soul was created to be free and happy. Any constraint for the soul equals death.

The freer the soul is, the happier we will be. We'll live our emotions more intensely and we'll fall in love with life. We'll rejoice in love more.

An awakened soul is an open gate to God and its key is in speaking and living in the spirit of the truth.

5. The belief that God is for us, with us and not against us.

Let's renounce being afraid of God. Let's give up on every fear of acting, of enjoying life. People always believe that it is not good to do certain things, they always believe that a thing that brings joy and pleasure to its soul is a sin. I know many people like this.

If only we'd acknowledge how much joy God is offering us in this world, with all its goods and all its experiences, then we'd not be afraid to live our lives anymore.

Forgetting about God is the real sin. It's a sin not to love God, it's a sin to judge God. People think that God is judging them, but in fact, they are the ones judging God.

God is never judgmental.

By saying that he is judging us and that He is punishing us, or by saying that He doesn't like certain things, people are judging Him. By blaming ourselvesfor many unimportant things, that seem important only to us, we are judging God.

Most people have the belief that in order to reach God you need to give up on life. In my courses, I've met people who said that they were afraid of a total communion with God because they still want to enjoy life. They don't want to isolate themselves because they were feeling the youth and power in them and they believed that life still had so many things to offer them.

But surprisingly, God also wants us to enjoy life.

It's wrong to think that once you are in communion with God, your life hasended. That you need to retreat to a hermitage or cave and till the end of your life, all you have to do is pray and meditate.

Most of the people who attained illumination, holiness, salvation or liberation - whatever we might like to call it - remained in isolation till they discovered who they really were. The moment they became one with God, they stopped being isolated. They returned to the world and rejoiced in its beauty just like others.

What is the meaning of enjoying life? For some it is drinking, smoking, having sex, going to parties, living a good life, travelling, having a nice home, eating good food or becoming a celebrity... Is there something else on that list?

God won't take any of these away from us. If a liberated being is not drinking alcohol anymore, that is because he doesn't feel the need for it. He will experience another sort of drunkenness, a Divine one. People resort to alcohol in order to run away from this world. Like an ostrich, they will bury their head in the sand believing that they are apart from the rest of the world. Once sober, when their heads are out again, they get scared and they start drinking again, so that they won't see it anymore.

That's because they are not seeing the beauty of this world.

It's the same for people who take drugs.

But a man who knows God will see the beauty of this world precisely because this whole world is God.

Many spiritual paths prohibit alcohol but in the life of Jesus Christ, wine is present. The wine was not present only at the wedding at Cana in Galilee, when Jesus transformed water into wine. He didn't say to the people then: *Stop now, you've had enough, don't drink a sip more! Drink just water!* Throughout His life He had wine with the people during their meals and feasts. And these people would say that they felt another type of drunkenness, a sweet drunkenness, unlike the one that one feels with alcohol. That was in fact beatitude.

It was really the beatitude of the communion with God, because they were in His presence then.

As for the Last Supper, Lord Jesus used wine and not water or juice, saying:

Drink, this is My blood!

During each celebration of the Resurrection, we receive holy bread and wine. On Easter, during the Midnight Mass, Christians will receive the Light and, together with it, holy wine. It's a wine of the best quality and He who donates it to the church isconsidered to have given a great offering to God.

It's not a problem to be sipping from an alcoholic drink occasionally, but if that becomes an escape from this world filled with the presence of God, then it is such a pity, because you won't be able to see Him. You are not with Him anymore. By placing your mind in the mists of alcohol, you'll be running away from something that you are in fact searching for. By getting inebriated, people feel better, happier. But actually, they are hiding from the world they live in, claiming happiness is not out there but only in the intoxication when, in fact, their soul is searching for the drunkenness of the communion with God.

Restlessly, our soul is searching for God. People always try to find happiness, hoping it will be in a victory, in love, in a material thing, a trip or a realisation. Once they attain it, the happiness lasts for a few days till a terrible unhappiness returns. Because the soul cannot bear unhappiness, a new search will start for another thing, another love, another realisation and so on. By knowing God, you realise that your searches stop in His pure happiness.

Once you've found God, you've found everything. In Him resides all realisation, all the fulfilments, all the loves, all the riches and all the possible joys.

Nobody can say that a liberated being is losing his senses and the joy of living. On the contrary, he is living everything with intensity. Each moment is whole, each moment is immense happiness.

They are also enjoying delicious, well-cooked food because they sense in its flavour the sublime flavour of God. They also are enjoying what is beautiful - the scent of flowers, the sound of music, the touch of love or of the wind. Their senses are more active, more receptive because in everything, they feel God's presence.

God doesn't mind. He is all these, He is all there is.

By thinking that they have to let go of everything, people aren't really desiring to reach God. So, they will taste a bit of everything: a bit of life's joys, but not too much so that they don't upset God, and a bit of God, as much as needed so He would help and protect us. This is also the reason why most people go to church or belong to a spiritual community. So people have fun, go to parties, have love relationships and then the guilt makes them run home, where they are safe and there they start praying for forgiveness because they had fun. People move fromone extreme to the other without finding the balance, the middle point where everything is at an arm's length.

Anyone would recognise that, because that's where we are now, as humanity.

On the one hand, the mind is saying: *It's forbidden!* On the other hand, the soul is crying for freedom and joy.

Man has not yet found a way to integrate everything into his Being.

If, whenever the soul craves for a joy or a pleasure, the mind would say: *There, in that pleasure God resides,* then it would be easier to find the balance point.

Experience joy in everything because there you will find God.

Taste it, savour it, satiate your eyes and senses but never forget, not even for a moment, that God is there.

By doing this for a short while, your mind will become purer, your soul will know how to choose and the communion with God will become deeper and deeper.

Of course, I am not saying this to killers, rapists, thieves and all the other people who are involved in performing wretched deeds. I am not encouraging them. I am addressing the normal human society we are a part of.

Either way, criminals and the like too will come to repent their deeds and will transform once they understand that God is in everything there is. If they steal, they are stealing from God, if they rape or murder, they are doing these things to God, if they cheat, they are cheating on God and so on.

God is not in a distant place, busy with His things so He won't see what we are doing. He is more present in our life than we imagine.

Enjoy everything, lovingly and completely, but always remember that God is in everything.

6. God is love, He is the love that nurtures this world.

All those who have had a vision of God have said that He is Love or that He is Light or even both.

The closer we get to Him, the more we are able to feel His great unconditional love. You will inexplicably feel enveloped by love.

Our beings are formed by different, other bodies than just the physical one that we are able to see and feel. Just like blood is flowing through the veins of our physical body, so does energy flow through our subtle bodies. The energy flows towards some energetic centres and, at the same time, it also flows from centres or energy sources. I won't explain these in detail because you can easily find information about all this on the web or in other books. They are also known as wheels of energy or chakras. One of these chakras, the fourth, is named Anahata and is the centre of love. Those who have this centre well activated and full of energy experience equal love towards all people, towards all of creation and believe that love has no conditions.

One of the methods of discovering God is to enter into this centre of love. It is the so-called heart-centred meditation. The deeper we dive into our love centre, the closer we get to God. By persevering with our meditations, contemplations or prayers in this centre, we are entering deeper and deeper into a space that exists in our spiritual heart and where, sooner or later, we will meet God. It's unbelievable how we search for God so desperately in so many places, thinking He might be in a remote heaven where we will get to in the after-life, when in reality, He is so near.

All those who have found God, have found Him here and not somewhere else.

That's the source of all these sayings that we might hear:

If you can't find God inside You, you won't find Him anywhere else.

As it is above, so it is below.

Know yourself and you will know the whole universe.

Man was made in the resemblance of God.

Over time, many discovered God and all of them say the same thing.

It's about time we start believing them. It's about time to open our eyes and to start searching for God inside us and not elsewhere.

God resides in the centre of love, God is the centre of love. God is all the love that exists in the world.

A loving man is a good man; he is altruistic, full of compassion and so on. So how could God be someone who punishes us, He who is expressing love through His existence?

We are afraid of punishments, we are afraid that we did wrong and we won't be forgiven. But God, through the love He is, is also forgiveness.

7. Together with life, He gave us freedom, that's how much He loves us.

Because we can't believe we have so much freedom, we are tying ourselves, we are creating conditions and restrictions. We suffocate as we bind ourselves with so many imaginary strings and when our soul cannot take it anymore, it starts to cry out for freedom. That is the start of our path to **liberation**. It ends when we regain what we had all along - what God gave us from the beginning.

He will let us choose what we are doing. He won't make plans for us, He won't impose anything on us; He won't scold us, judge us or be upset with us.

He won't say: *I'll love you only if... I'll bestow my grace on you only if...*

You'll receive my blessing only if...

This free will He gave us is a proof of the freedom we are blessed with since the beginning. Then why would people think that we shouldn't do this, that or the other and so on?

God gave us freedom and we, humans, are the ones always setting conditions.

We want liberation and God created us free. Despite that, all the known paths to liberation are full of conditions.

We always think we need to do something in order to receive something else.

This mind of ours is a great trickster.

We actually have everything, that's why we are enjoying such a great freedom.

We are gifted with everything, we can benefit fully from all there is. Inside us exists all that there is outside us. Then, why are there so many conditions?

Why are there so many limits?

It's funny how people want to put boundaries on everything in order to possess them. The more boundaries that are set, the less we possess.

God created this wonderful world and we have it at our disposal. See nature, the mountains, the rivers and lakes, the grass, the flowers, the woods, the oceans, the animals, the sun, the plenitude of scents, the soft breeze... Our Earth, a small planet in this Universe, even smaller when compared with the multitude of existing universes, has so many free, boundless places. Man tries to set boundaries for everything and puts up property signs.

It's funny how we are building fences, owning properties or setting borders that we are so strict with. We never think that we are One, that there are no differences amongst us and that we won't take anything with us to our graves.

More than that, no matter how hard people strive to include and bind everything, they can't be successful. There is so much of this beautiful place that was decorated by the Divine Artist and where we are free to go for a walk and take delight in the beauty surrounding us.

It is said we are on the way to Satya Yuga, a new important age of humankind, a golden age, but this time the golden refers to the spiritual.

By the way, *Satya* means Truth, so even speaking and living in the spirit of the truth will come together in this new age.

Everybody's freedom is increasing as we get closer to this new era. Yes, there are borders, but we are free to travel everywhere in the world. That was not the case hundredyears ago. Now we also have different options, like planes and other fast modes of transport.

The internet gives us access to information from all over the world, no matter the field of interest. This is one of God's greatest gifts of freedom. There are new ways of communicating directly, rapidly, with people from all over the world via the internet. We can not only speak, but we can see each other. Were all of these created against God's will? Has God allowed all this and why? Through these communication methods we are starting to merge, to become One.

It is said that the future will be one of a single religion. People are already starting to understand that there is only one God.

We are uniting our souls and we will become one.Freedom was given to us, it belongs to us, we just need the courage to use it.

8. The fastest path to liberation is by loving God. In exchange for our love He will burn our karma.

As I said in teaching number 7, because of His great love for us, God offered us freedom, as a gift, along with life. Now we need to go all the way back and love him in return – by loving Him we will regain our freedom.

All we have to do is to love Him.

I dare to say that this Path of Love to God is the most rapid and direct path to liberation. Nothing compares to it, no matter which technique we follow - meditation, ascesis, fasting, a pilgrimage or prayers.

All these techniques are of help; they are steps or crutches that gradually awaken this love for God in our soul.

Armed with the knowledge that if we do it - that is love God - would be our greatest realisation, as humans, as spirits.

Once, during a conversation on a similar topic with someone who had been on thespiritual path for over twenty years, someone had asked them:

What does it mean to love God?

If you'd been asked that, your reply would be: to pray, to do asanas, to meditate, to engage in spiritual practice, to go to church, to the temple, to do good deeds, to love other people, to help the poor and so on.

But all these are just steps towards loving God.

It's easy to love a human being, an animal or any other thing because you see them.

But how can you love something you do not see?

We are going around in a circle.

Yes. It's a great secret.

The masters say that God chooses the moment when He will bestow His grace upon us and they also say that if we take even one small step towards Him, He will take thousandsteps towards us.

What does that mean?

In this freedom that God has given to us, He's also included the freedom to choose the moment of our liberation as easily as we, humans can choose the moment of our death.

God offered us access to His Power.

Yes, I can make a choice.

How will I do that?

Jesus taught us this when He said: *If you love your mother, your father, your brothers or your children more than you love Me, then you don't love me at all.*

It's our choice to give God the first place in our life, in our heart.

And for many, it's not an easy choice. In the course of my teachings, I have observed it several times. When I tell my students about this, tears start running downtheir faces. They say that they cannot put aside the love they feel for their children. I can expound several theories - that the love for God includes the love for family or that God resides in them too and so on, but it's all about feeling. Many say: *But I do love God*, and then I say: *Yes, but is it just with half of your heart?*

So we come back to the question – how do we love God?

Only your soul can find the answer to this question. Wishing for it, searching for it, at a point you'll be able to find that total love for God. You will simply feel it; you cannot talk about it because there are no words to describe such heavenly love.

As I said, the choice is ours. We choose to love Him and then, when the time comes, we will know how to love Him. When we truly love Him, an outpouring of Grace will instantly bestow upon us, continuously.

This Grace won't come when God wants it, as they say. This Grace is continuously bestowing, it is always there. It's we who, at a certain time, will open our hearts to receive it. Thus, we are the ones choosing the moment of our liberation.

The masters, the teachers of spirituality, the priests, the initiates, the gurus or any other human being wishing to teach others about God are playing a very important part here. There are so many cases when the disciples are not told that it is so easy to reach God - that is either because they don't know it or because there are other reasons.

A disciple will trust his master completely and his path to liberation could be so rapid if the Truth would be told to Him.

Unfortunately, there are so many spiritual schools and courses where newer and newer spiritual information isgiven to the student, only to overload his mind.

If for a year you keep saying the same thing over and over again, if you directly transmit it and you make him feel the truth that you are saying, at the end, the student will understand and will make it his or her truth.

We live in a time when we're bombarded with information. This is a good thing, allowing us to choose the path that best suits us.

In my opinion, the first step would be to wish from the bottom of our hearts to fall in love with God and only then can we load our mind with tons of information, if we really need it.

If you ask a liberated being, a Christian saint, a Sufi mystic or a realised soul from another religion, *what he can tell you about God,* he would say that He is Love and Light.

He will talk out of experience, because this is how they see and feel Him from their meetings with Him. Each of them would say that the most important thing is to love God. Each of them would say that they were in love with Him.

After they experienced Him, they felt the need to share their happiness and to help others to feel Him.

That is why it is important for us to ask for their help, guidance, advice and inspiration.

Jesus said: ***I am the Path, the Truth and Life.***

He who knows the Truth will always utter the truth. If Jesus said ***I am the Path,*** that means that He can lead us on the path to God and take us to Him.

We have to call Him and to pray to Him to help us live the state of permanently being in love with God. We can also invoke every saint or liberated being. They would be very happy to help us as well; the same goes for the Angels and the liberated spirits that are now in the world beyond.

I previously mentioned that we can even choose the moment of our death. It is so. If God offered us the freedom to choose liberation, why wouldn't He offer us the freedom to choose when we incarnate and when we leave?

At somepoint, we are asking to die. We've had enough with life, with suffering and all that we do, so we say: *I'd rather die than continue like this… I'm tired of this illness and I don't want to live like this anymore so it would be better if I'd die…*

By repeating this, no matter if it's in a loud voice or just in our mind, by feeling this desire, death is coming closer. When we call for it repeatedly, it will come, won't it? We often do so unconsciously. Sometimes, and that is even worse, we do it in a half-aware state: *I know I'll die young, I know I won't get to be 50, I know I'll have an accident, I know I won't have the chance to grow old…*and so on.

Oh Lord, and how many other thoughts like these we have! How much harm we are doing to ourselves! Nobody is harming us, nobody is punishing us – we are the ones attracting all that is happening in our life.

Someone asked me: *Well, what is God's part in this plan?*

The answer is simple: He is respecting our freedom and our choices.

God exists, we are not excluding Him, because we can't. We are part of Him, we are one with Him. His love for us is so great, that if we wish for something and we ask for it, He will give it to us.

God does not refuse the True desires of our soul.

Many times, we think we want something when, in fact, our soul desires something else. God answers the soul and not the mind or our social obligations or necessities. God is always talking with our soul and is always listening to its needs.

Let's talk about illnesses too. A person will become sick and will heal whenever they want. The mind is blackmailing the soul. If by getting sick we get someone's attention, then the soul will desire the illness. Whenever we are feeling lonely and unloved, we are subconsciously desiring to get sick, either to get someone's attention or to leave this world.

This subject will be covered later. I just wanted to mention that an illness is not a punishment nor an inheritance from our ancestors, as it is said. Healing is in our hands.

Returning to this chapter's subject, the love for God will burn all of our karma, be it negative or positive. It will break the tormenting karmic ties and also the happy ones. We will be able to rejoice in everything that is beautiful in a state of freedom.

All our karma will dissolve only through this state of love for God.

Beyond that, let's remember that God is the first one to enjoy freedom. His freedom is boundless. We are made in His resemblance.

It's funny when a religious movement or a sect appears and says that it is only by following them that you will be able to find God, it is only within their sect that true God resides and you won't find Him anywhere else. Let's be serious. If someone can show us a single place in this entire creation where God does not exist, then that person must be unique!

Just as it is with love, a divine messenger, a prophet, a special being that has had the revelation of Divinity will appear. Then, the others who didn't sense it will create a system out of it. The system will create boundaries. Suffocated, lacking freedom, people won't be able to find God there. But they will stay out of fear... They believe that it is only there that they canfind Him, that's what they have beentold. God cannot be forced into a system, into a mantra or into some strict, suffocating rules.

The person who thinks this lives in a state of great illusion.

How could you enclose God, who is Freedom itself, Infinity itself, who is boundless?

Some will say: *Yes, but some rules have to exist, otherwise people will act foolishly.* The rules are made by man and not by God.

If we have to think of rules sent by God, then those would be: love, humanity and common sense. Actually, it will be just one: Love. Because he who truly loves acts in a humane manner and always with a lot of common sense.

JOURNAL

After that angelic healing, I succumbed to the temptation of taking care of the house and so, the next day I didn't write.

At the end of the day, because I hadn't respected my promise, I became sick, as before.

A new day in bed and with little mobility.

Another day had passed and I felt I was once again entering into that zero point where I can choose to heal. I asked God to forgive me and to heal me again.

Amazingly, God healed me!

But who could stop me from doing my chores?

I wrote for two days and then again, I started to do some housework.

In a few hours, I was again in bed.

It seemed as if I had no choice. I had to finish the book before doing anything else.

As I was lying in bed, thinking, an idea crossed my mind: God must have observed that I had decided to finish the book, so maybe I should unconditionally ask Him to heal me. It's obvious I also have other things to do.

Let's try that.

So I prayed again for healing, this time without conditions.

God is really very kind to us! He healed me again and since that moment, the problem hasn't returned even though I haven't written anything for two days in a row. I really think that this grace of healing is a powerful expression of God's love and compassion.

Whenever I ask for something, He gives it immediately, completely and with an immense, unconditional love.

A condition like a herniated disk is difficult to cure and there I was, cured three times in a week. This healing process was in itself a spiritual experience.

I'm amazed. Thank You, Lord!

I will say this now so I that I needn't return to this story.

I have seen how God can cure us unconditionally if we have faith in Him. Maybe to some of you this will seem like a child's game, but it's not so. It takes great faith to be able to heal yourself in such a manner. I just wanted to let you see how God acts and the ease with which He fulfils our wishes.

Till I finished writing the book, there were again some warnings whenever I stopped writing for any length of time. At that time, some pains would appear.

But they were not big, I was never confined to bed again. I was just being warned that I need to continue.

Nothing was working, no type of treatment.

All was in God's hand and He was pushing me from behind so that I'd finish the book.

This continued till I finished the book and once the book was completed, the healing was complete too.

It was a very beautiful Divine Game.

Thank You for this experience.

9. God is working with us in everything we do.

We have the impression that God can be 'bothered' only for important things…but that's not true. He desires to live our life together with us. He wishes to be involved in all aspects of our life, even if at first, they seem insignificant. From His point of view, nothing is insignificant. Both big things and small things have equal importance for Him. It's no use imagining Him in a distant paradise from where He is looking down on us and where you don't have access to Him, nor where our voices can reach Him.

So let's not go to Him only when we have a difficult problem at work or in the family or when we have a health problem.

Let's go to Him when we are doing small things also, like, for example, when we go to pick some apples from the orchard.

As I've already said, God doesn't live in a distant paradise. He is with us and next to us every moment. We are practically ignoring Him when we are going to pick apples because He is always with us, even in the orchard.

He is with us every moment, working together with us.

The moment we become conscious of His presence next to us, WE WILL NO LONGER BE ABLE TO EXCLUDE HIM FROM OUR LIVES.

We will no longer be able to eat without thinking of Him because He is there with us, at the table. We won't be able to clean the house anymore without thinking of His presence there, and in love making too, He will be there and we won't be able to do it without acknowledging His presence.

We'll have to get used to this idea of Him being present in every moment and every action of our life and it's not right to ignore Him.

God wants to live our lives.

If we'll allow Him, we will be aware of His presence and we will understand the meaning of the act of consecration – we will truly abandon our ego and we will let Him act. We won't be able to ignore Him. If we are to perform another action without the consecration, it is like we are turning our backs on Him and we are saying: *No, You stay there, I'll do this alone...* or *Don't come with me, You stay home while I go on this trip* and so on. This is a great illusion.

If we are really aware of how present God is in our lives, we would be enchanted. On many occasions, He is really doing everything in our place and we are like simple guests, invited to live our own lives.

10. The Divine Will.

When we understand the true meaning of the consecration and that God is present by our side in every moment, we also understand the true sense of the Divine Will.

Most of the time, when we hear that we must accomplish the Divine Will, we get tense and scared because our mind immediately triggers the idea that our will is separated from the Divine Will, the latter seeming a restriction.

You must know that it isn't so.

God always fulfils our wishes.

There were many occasions, in your life also, when you would hardly think about something and it was realised. If we pay a little attention to what goes on with us and our lives, we will notice the speed with which God is fulfilling our wishes.

Then we can ask, amazed: *But God, what are You doing? Who are You, my Master or my servant?!*

Yes, it's true, it might seem rude to address Him like that, but how then is it possible to receive so much importance from our Good God, our Heavenly Father, He who comprises everything and takes care of all the Universe and the entire creation?

It's true. A true lord, leader, president, master, guru or teacher is one who serves his subjects, disciples or students in a totally unconditional manner, as God does – without judging, threatening or punishing and by respecting your free will. God does the same thing, He who is the Supreme Master, Teacher, Leader.

In a spiritual society, as Satya Yuga will be, so it will happen.

This is how God is. I feel like calling Him Good God but I won't repeat myself too often, so that I do not bore you dear reader. But He really is like this: a Being of immeasurable kindness.

Whenever you do wrong and feel guilty, you pray to receive God's forgiveness. If your soul is even just a little bit open, you will be able to feel God's disarming love. He forgave you from the moment you did wrong. He never judged you and He welcomes you into His arms again and again, with all the kindness in the world.

If we start to love Him and have a relationship with Him, then we will start to understand Him. Our will will become more and more similar to His Will, until they become identical.

We believe that our wishes should be just spiritual ones. But it's not like that. God did not create us to see how we are suffering fromlack, fromhunger, frustrated that there are so many joys and beauties in this world (who created those and why?) but not daring to touch them because they arenot spiritual. God is in all, then it goes without saying that all is spiritual.

He gave us all the riches of this world and He wishes us to fully enjoy them.

If people have personal desires, the spiritually inclined will say that those are the desires of our ego. But why does God, who is Spirituality Itself, fulfil these wishes?

Most of the time, that which at first seems to come out of an immense egoism is a necessary experience in our life, transforming itself into a spiritual experience.

That relativity is great and it's applicable in everything. What is good for some is bad for others. What is true for some is false for others and so on.

So we need to leave things around us as they are, without judging them. If we want things to transform in our environment we must start the transformation in our minds.

Once we are close enough to God, our will become identical to His Will.

The speed at which our wishes are fulfilled can be the barometer that estimates how close we are to God.

For our will to become one with His Will, the fastest and the best way is to love Him. Through this love for Him, an intimate connection is created, which will be the catalyst of the Oneness of our will with His Will. Of course, all this will happen in time, naturally, without any effort or sacrifice.

As this love relationship with God gets more and more intimate, a certain spiritual maturity will also appear. At first, like a child, you will ask for all sorts of toys. You are still frustrated thanks tonot playing enough in your childhood. At that time, you didn't know how to ask. After you've had enough of that play time, you then start to ask for other things, according to the level of your maturity.

Oh, stop! Don't judge yourselves. In God's eyes, it doesn't matter if you're a child or a mature being. Our minds always want us to be seen as adults.

Try.Experiment and you will see that you will receive all, no matter if it's a toy or a seemingly important 'grown up' thing.

God gives to us, but why does He?

Because, His Will is the same as our will.

There is no more separation of the ego, the ego is gone, it is no longer between you and Him. It becomes such a wonderful and delightful pleasure to fulfil His Will.

More than that, think that at a point, through this union with Him in the heart, which will spontaneously appear in your loving relationship, you will feel that He gave you everything. The whole Universe is His gift for you… What else can you wish for? If you wish for it, then it must be a necessity for surviving in this plane (even relaxation and fun are necessary) and you will rapidly receive it because it's all yours and it's like you are pluckingit from your garden. There is no effort in attracting the things that belong to you.

You utter your wish and it becomes a command. The Angels of God will fulfil it because you have all the rights to receive anything that is part of this creation.

Believe me, once there, in this state, you will only wish for things that are already yours.

Remember this important aspect: when our will is one with the Will of God, then all our wishes are fulfilled.

Always, with no exception.

11. Each person has his well-established place in the Divine Creation.

The great Universe is created from the smaller universes that we are creating. Each thought, idea or state is generating something. It is creating. We are really creators without even knowing it. It would still be good to know it because we would pay more attention to what we are creating.

We can never say that someone is harming us. It is our negative karma who found that person to manifest itself through. That person is just an instrument that is fulfilling our thoughts. We are generating the universe in which we are living and if someone is harming us, that person is just doing what we have created.

Often, we arrive in certain places just to say or do something that will change a person's destiny. This is not coincidence. It was a necessity for us to be there at that point.

The universe we live in is created by us. We generate it and we create it continuously through our thoughts, intentions and deeds.

Through our thoughts and intentions, we are continuously asking and God will grant us all those wishes.

If we become aware we will pay more attention to our thoughts.

Let me give you an example. Once I was returning home with someone by car and we were having a conversation so that the time would pass. There was no connection between us so we had no common grounds on which to begin a dialogue.

At some point, that person said: *I plan to go to the US and swim with the dolphins. There is a specially arranged gulf and there are well-trained instructors so you can do that. I've always wanted to swim with the dolphins! It must be fascinating.*

I answered politely: *Yes, it must be interesting,* but my soul said:*How beautiful! How beautiful it is to be swimming with the dolphins...*

Then the conversation jumped to a different topic and after that the dolphins never appeared in my mind. But that favourable state was an energy I oriented in a specific direction and also an uttered subconscious wish. I was not aware, because at that time I knew that it was an expensive trip and the money for it was out of my reach. So I gave up even dreaming about it.

But would you believe me when I tell you that just two months later I was swimming with the dolphins?

We went to Israel and amongst the many places we visited there, we arrived at the Red Sea, in Eilat. There a gulf was arranged for diving and swimming with the dolphins...and there was also a giant turtle and lots of fishes and other aquatic attractions.

I swam in there and I enjoyed everything the placehad to offer without thinking that it was afulfilment of what I had asked for a while ago, unconsciously.

The same happens in our life too.

The emotion we add to a thought, be it good or bad, is the energy that will bring it towards fulfilment. It helps us fulfil our dreams or to create our destiny or the life we live or the universe we exist in.

So we shouldn't be surprised atthe life we have because it is totally created by us.

Whenever socialisation and relating occurs, then the two people are agreeing, consciously or unconsciously, to create that universe together. It's not a chance that we are meeting, that we all end up in the same place or that we are experiencing similar emotions or events.

The appearance of someone with a role in our life, be it positive or negative, is in direct connection with our thought and intentions. That person is an instrument, fulfilling what we were thinking.

The most difficult part is accepting that we created the negative events in our life: accidents, illnesses, painful breakups, etc.

Bu that is the truth - we created them.

Maybe once, in a relationship, we lost our faith in the other, the love was gone, the relationship stopped evolving and all that was left was a great attachment. A breakup follows inevitably. If the pure love that was there in the beginning had remained, together with all the trust in the loved one and all the metamorphosis, the relationship would have lasted forever. There is also our own lack of confidence: *I don't think he/she can love me because I am not perfect, I have all the defects, he/she is so beautiful and smart...*and so much more. Our lack of confidence in the relationship's future will lead to a sure breakup. The moment the first thought ofthis relationship not lasting has been planted in our minds, the flower of breakup has been planted too.

So it is with every event in our life, good or bad.

Where is God's role in all this?

God is pure love and, as I said before, He grants our every wish out of His immense love for us.

The moment the first discomfort appears in a relationship, either caused by the self or by the other, that evil will grow until the happiness is gone. All that remains is the attachment that we often confuse with love.

God is separating us because He cannot stand to see us suffer.

If it were up to us, we'd stay there till extermination. We'd suffer terribly, happiness being thousands of kilometres away, only for the sake of 'love'.

Because we misunderstand it. There is no suffering in love. Where there is suffering, the love is over.

So, all we have to do is to understand that what is going on with us, good or bad, was requested by us, consciously or unconsciously and it is fulfilled by God.

Whatever will be, whatever will happen, we need to have faith that it is for our own good.

Each person is in the place they should be. There is no inferior work or superior work, no pleasant or unpleasant activity, something nice or something abject for God. It just is and it is an answer to a request.

Those who are simple workers might believe that they have a job on the lowest part of the social scale and the ones with important positions or the rich ones might look down on them.

What a big illusion!

If those workers didn't exist, to work till exhaustion, would we still have bread or other food on the table, chairs to sit on and other furniture, blankets to cover ourselves, clothes to wear and many other things that are useful in our lives? If it were not for the singers, the musicians, the artists - who delight our senses - who would help us relax when we are tense and need to regenerate?

People are judging and pointing fingers at one another all the time but all of us are Angels where we are, because we all are bringing a service to the society in which we live.

The one cleaning the streets shouldn't feel inferior to the one who is a big director, president or businessman because these so-called 'superior' people wouldn't feel so good if they didn't live in a clean city. Each person has his or her well-established role in this world, chosen by himself or herself and each is important where he/she is.

12. Happiness is when you love God and you feel loved by Him.

People are always in the pursuit of happiness. This is the reason why many choose to satisfy their senses, to fulfil their desires, to have many experiences, to always be searching for something. That moment or those minutes or days when we rejoice over what we've achieved or felt are just drops of happiness that will soon melt in a puddle of big disappointment.

We see that happiness is not lasting but we still crave for it. So we are always searching for it in something else, forever.

We experience a plenary happiness when we fall in love. It is said that you can love but as for falling in love, it happens only when God wishes it. Then we are feeling His love and this is what makes us very happy. But most don't recognise this Divine Love in those moments and they turn all their attention and gratitude towards the person they are in love with. Then, in those first moments of falling in love, we don't see the defects of the other because the Divine Perfection is all there is. God is perfect and that is what we are seeing. We are happy and we feel like flying because we are really in love with God. If we could see that then, the state of being in love would never end because, as God is infinite, so will our love be. But we donot usually see God there - we are seeing the being through which God has manifested, awakening such a love in them. Each time we fall in love, we receive an invitation from God to love Him. By not seeing and knowing that, all our love will go towards a person who, gradually, because of the desires and attachments, will leave the divine perfection and will manifest its ego. Then the other one sees them with all their defects. But the agreement was already made. From the egoistic desire to keep God only for himself, they have been tied through matrimony. But God belongs to all of us. So that can't be. Then, *after the state of being in love is gone,* remains the love. It's not a bad

Semida David

thing if that would last, but the human desire of having a love relationship with God, of tasting, of indulging again and again inthe Divine Love, will leave the relationship searching for a new occasion to fall in love.

Our soul is programmed to be in love with God. Otherwise we are not happy. We are suffering, we are tormented.

If we are able to fall in love with God, our soul will live a happiness without an equivalent. It will be happy because it will do what it needs to do. This love relationship that will appear between us and God will be the spring of our eternal happiness. We will experience a happiness for no particular reason, which is unconditional, that will spring again and again from our soul. Whether we do or don't have money, riches, relationships, success, we will always have the happiness inside us that, once discovered, will be never lost.

It might seem like a tale - what I am saying now - but each of us has this happiness hidden in our souls, inside our spiritual heart.

When you are able to open that door, something amazing will happen.

The secret of happiness is the Love of God.

13. The communion with God brings us a state of complete fulfilment.

This state when we feel God is in our heart comes together with a state of unconditional love that will bring us great happiness. It then has,therefore, a state of fulfilment that we experience on every level of our being. It is a spiritual fulfilment, but also an effective one, a material one and it reflects itself in every aspect of our existence.

At first it comes as a complete fulfilment in your heart. Even if you are a have or have not, even if you are rich or poor, even if you are among other people or alone, in your heart you will feel a state of having it all and not needing anything else.

Of course, this state also attracts total happiness. You are simply happy. Maybe you have or you don't, maybe you have no clothes to wear or nothing to eat, but the happiness in your soul doesn't disappear.

The inner state of fulfilment will attract, through resonance, an outer fulfilment too.

If you live as though all the world is yours, it's obvious that soon you will attract in your life all that you need, all that you are wishing for and even more.

In this way, you will know God's kindness and generosity, which are also unconditional.

Once you finally attain this state, you will never lose it.

God, once discovered (won) is ours forever.

Once we win God, He will take us in His care.

14. Once we discover God, it is for eternity.

Either way, Godis never separated from us. We are the ones separating from Him because we forget about Him. Forgetting deepens if we make the wrong choices. We have experiences - that's not a problem because Godrespects our choices. There is no need to judge, but at somepoint, forgetting becomes so deep that wedeny His existence. Then our soul starts tomiss Him and we begin to search for Him. It's then when we go to church or to the temple - we are searching for spiritual paths, for priests, masters or gurus, believing that they will help us find Him again. We forget that He is always with us and the role of the priests and the spiritual masters is to remind us of that. We can do that alone too; it's just that we don't know how. We have everything in us, even this chance and this capacity to remember where we came from and who we are.

The great part is that once we rediscover God, this meeting will be eternal. The soul remembers the suffering from the separation and won't make the same choices again. This time, the choice will be to be as close to God as possible.

This is valid beyond death too, in between the two worlds and in ourfuture lives, if we choose to return tothis world.

Once we reach Him, it will be forever.

15. Once reached, God takes you under His care.

This subchapter perfectlyfollows the previous one. I said then that the soul will make a choice towards the good, towards love, towards God. What is important to remember here is that we are no longer alone. Once we make the effort to return, God is the one who won't ever let us fall.

Once back home, the wandering son won't leave anymore and, at the same time, God won't ever let him leave.

Maybe we are still weak and we tend to make the wrong choices, but from now on God is the one changing our direction each time.

He is sublimating our negative states, He is next to us when we feel it's difficult and He is telling us that it is not important to pay so much attention to aspects that we don't like. Even without noticing, we are taken out of our negative states as soon as they set in. The same applies to problems, troubles, misunderstandings and any other life situation or soul-related situation that seems difficult.

He does that for us, without us having to ask for it. Once we reach Him, He takes care of all our problems and all we have to do is to live life happy and serene. He will take care of everything.

16. The communion with God grants us perfect health.

By being one with Him and Him being perfect, we can't be anything else but perfect.

The happiness that we instantly feel when we are in communion with Him allows the free flow of energies through our body.

Lately, people talk more and more about the subtle causes of illness and about treating the illness by treating its cause first. It is known that the mind generates everything, including sickness. All the negative, obsessive, destructive thoughts we might have will block the free flow of energies through our body. The energy will get stuck in certain areas, corresponding to the thought. We will be stuck on a negative idea that will create a blockage in the physical body. The longer we remain stuck, the longer the blockage. The energies that ensure the good functioning of the body through their flow are not allowed to go through there and, in time, that will lead to the apparition of an illness. If we could go through this path in reverse, from the sickness to the mind, so, in other words, we get to understand the exact thoughts or obsessions that create the energetic blockage and thus the illness, we would be able to cure ourselves without needing any treatment.

Through this continuous happiness, which is a result of the communion with God, the energies are flowing freely through our body and sickness cannot appear. If it exists, it will heal and if you happen to become sick because, at somepoint, you made the wrong choice, then it will heal very quickly.

17. God excitedly awaits us and He is always ready to receive us.

You might be wondering: *God excited?*

Yes, excited. We know we were created in His resemblance. If we have so many types of emotions, why can't God have emotions too?

God is always waiting for us with the excitement of a man waiting for his lover.

It's that emotion of reunion, as the one who reaches Him feels he is back home.

The joy of returning to God is greater for Him than for us, because we have just arrived after wandering fora long way but He knows and He is waiting for us since we left.

18. There is nothing we need to do. God does everything.

As I said before, God loves us very much and wants us to be happy and fulfilled. So, He will take care of everything in order to ensure that we are happy and fulfilled.

The more we worry about our lives, the less trust we have in God.

And I mean trust, not faith.

It is possible that we have faith in Him, but because of our education or simply because we don't know, we don't have trust in Him.

If we trust Him, our only concern would be that our love for Him shouldgrow and for all the rest of the problems we face, we would be reassured, knowing that He takes care of us.

All our problems, as humans and as humanity, are quickly solved, with love and in the most favourable way by God Himself.

The key is to trust Him and let Him act.

Most of the time, before He can do anything, we intervene and make decisions related to our personal life.

Most of the time, we believe that we have to pray to God for peace, to avoid a catastrophe, for humanity's welfare. But we don't even think that the One to whom we are praying wants only good for us. He doesn't want a world with war or poverty or catastrophes in our life. It's not necessary to pray for all that. God watches over us and protects us always. We would be better off paying attention to our thoughts, our wishes and our deeds which attract these catastrophes.

Because He takes care of everything, all we have to do is live our life in joy, happiness and love for God.

Everything was created in the minutest detail so that we would be good.

Life is a feast and we were invited to it by God Himself. We need to enjoy all that is at our disposal and to abandon ourselves into His hands, completely trusting Him.

Everything relating to our life's security, our happiness and welfare is already sorted for us.

Then what is our purpose? you mightask me.

My answer is: if someone invites you to a holiday on a tropical island, all inclusive, with people to serve you and provide all that you need at your disposal, on arrival you would say you are in paradise. You won't demolish the hotel and start building a new one, you won't sew new bedding because you already have bedding that is nice and clean and you won't start to cook and wash the floor because there are people taking care of all thattoo.

So it is with the life that God prepared for us - He isthe first one at our disposal, listening to us, understanding our soul and serving us.

If we start to getbored with all this good fortune, then we become creative and we will say that the world that God created for us is not beautiful enough. So we will start building a hotel next to the one in which we are staying. A bigger and more beautiful one. We will have problems with the funds, with the employees, with the project and the necessary approvals and then we will start complaining about the problems and about how tough life is. Then, once we have built it, what would we do with it? We have to recover our investment. So we will start to worry about how to get clients. Then we will have to set prices for their stay there, in order to recover our investment. Then we will put a fence around it so that nobody cancome in without paying and we obtainthe property papers so that everybody will know it is ours and that they cannot take it from us. So we are creating a world that belongs to us in the world that God created. We will say that life is in our hands. Whenever we get into trouble we will pray to God to help us, without realising that He helps us each time we intend to do something. Without His help, we could not have made it.

In fact, we already have a hotel that was built for us and the same exists in real life. When we come here we have everything we need,assured by God.

People lose their trust in Him and then want to take life into their own hands.

On the contrary, we should detach ourselves and place ourselves into God's hands, trusting Him.

We are the ones complicating our life. We are where we are, in that situation, because we sought it, because we asked for it, because of the choices we made. There is nothing to complain about. We will resolveourtroubles just by trusting God.

We have faith but our trust is missing.

We want to sort everything, we believe that we should do everything.

He prepared for us a beautiful and fulfilling life, full of gifts and abundance. What we have to do is to trust Him.

19. God loves to laugh so we should trust Him, we should let Him sort all our problems and we should enjoy life.

We should laugh together with God. To roar in laughter as He does. It's not a sin to laugh, it's not a sin to be happy! The life God designed for us is full of joy. We should act like the children who laugh happily, knowing that their mother is taking care of everything.

Many see God as being serious and grave.

When they meditate with God they use songs that are serious, grave, with low tones or transcendental and astral music, thinking of God as being serious and not knowing how to joke. They see Him somewhere far away, in unreachable universes.

The only people that I am aware of that have a different vision of the Divine arethe Hindus. Their religious celebrations include dancing and singing. Their prayers are sung tohappy rhythms. God is a reason of happiness and joy for them.

In fact, this is God. All those who have felt Him and 'met' Him, experienced an inexplicable happiness afterwards. If all who knew Him, no matter their religion, live inhappiness that has no stringent rules, then why do others on the same path stick to the idea that in order to reach Him you must wear black, you must fast, you must isolate yourself, you mustn't laugh but mustbe grave and serious?

I reallydon't get that.

Although all religions have their saints and illuminated beings, only the Hindus have implemented that joy of the communion with God in their daily life.

Christians rejoice at Christmas and celebrate it with songs and joy and presents. Everyone looks forward to Christmas for this joy.

Then voices appear saying that we have drifted apart from the real meaning of Christmas, the Birth of Christ and that is something serious because He came into this world to take away our sins, to die on the cross for us.

Even Jesus was happy. Believe me, He was not sad during His earthly life.

You cannot be sad when you are one with God.

The communion with God brings the happiness that was given to us since birth.

You should laugh with all your heart and enjoy life because this is how we make God happy too.

There are so many wonderful things that he created for us. Look carefully at nature, see the people, see the new inventions that came to make our life easy. Let's enjoy them and the life we have and let's leave all our worries to God. If we trust Him, we will see, with surprise, that Hewill sort out everything rapidly and in the most favourable way possible for us.

20. One God for all of us.

We live in a society that is bringing together people from different religions. We get along perfectly until the subject of God comes along and then we frown, each one saying that their God is the true one.

It is so sad that a false idea can bring so much disagreement among people!

I've researched the mechanisms of societies a little and I've observed that every now and then, a messenger of God appears, awakening faith in humans and creating a path that would lead them to God. It is their path and they transmit it to others. There are many paths and all of them are taking us to the same, unique God.

The problem is not with them but with their disciples who haven't felt God and, in order not to lose the devotees, they create a system.

The more rigid the system is, the more it limits the freedom of the people, the more it controls their minds...and the more rules it has the more distant it is from God. This is what humans are doing. Those rules were not created by the divine messengers who started that path.

I don't want to upset anyone but if you study a little, you will see that all the messengers of God didnot create schools with rules and restrictions, huge temples or churches, hierarchical systems, etc. See the modesty in the lives of Jesus, Mahavira,

Buddha, Muhammad and many others who came to create a path.

Their ideas were simple and full of common sense and humanity.

All are saying the same thing because the Truth has the same source.

I received an immense grace through this Divine Guidance (that all have access to, without realising it) and at a point I had this dilemma: to which God should I pray? I have talked about this earlier in the book. I loved Jesus and I wouldn't have left Him for anything in the world. But whenI travelled to India, I discovered Shiva. I've seen that He too is answering and offering me spiritual gifts. I've seen that the Hindu path also led to God. I had the Christian God and the Hindu God. The states were similar. I meditated in mosques and temples and other religiousplaces and I felt that God was everywhere. It was just that my mind was still perplexed because of my education and because of the environment I lived in.

I was so tormented by this dilemma and I kept asking till the Divine answer came: *There is just one God, the same for everyone*. Only when He gave me the answer did I calm down, and I believed it. I didn't want to be mistaken and I'm sure you don't want that either.

Yes, God is One, only One and the same for all.

A time will come when everyone will realise this.

21. By loving God we become one with Him.

We arehis counterpart. We are the ones who complete Him in Hismanifestation. God brings plenitude in all aspects of our lives. One of the most important aspects that motivates our actions is the amorous one. This is not the best word to include all aspects, from the sexual one to what all of us are searching for: our other half, counterpart, ideal love. This implies we will find a person to complete us on all levels.

One of the reasons there are so many divorces and so much sexual freedom is that we are continually searching for that one person who willcomplete us on all levels. As a result, around 50% of the planet's population has had more than one relationship in their lifetime.

By failing to find what we are searching for and continuously being unfulfilled, we continue searching, in the hope that we will finally find the ideal love.

I've said previously that the love for God creates a state of fulfilment on all levels. Yes, it's true - even the need of the soul to reunite is solved by God if we win His heart.

Yes, reaching Him, or better said, discovering Him, needs some effort onour part, but once we achieve that we are rewarded.

Even this aspect of our life becomes sorted. We are loved by God as a lover. We begin to have a complete relationship with Him. He is our Father, our Friend, our Lover and our Husband. He becomes our ideal Love, the one we've been searching for lives after lives.

In Hinduism, the counterpart of Shiva (God) is Parvati.

Through the complete love that God is gives us, women will feel as loved and adored as Parvati Herself by her Beloved Shiva. Men will feel as loved and adored as Shiva Himself by His Beloved Parvati.

God is beyond the duality of sex or gender. No one can say precisely if God is a man or a woman. So for us, He is either man or woman, depending on our needs.

A woman who has attained a complete relationship with God will feel Him become the Ideal Lover. She will feel she is permanently loved, adored, caressed, she will receive spiritual and material gifts, she will always be understood, she won't ever be alone and she will also be erotically fulfilled.

Sexuality and our sexual organs are part of us and of our life. There is no point in skimming over this subject that is so much a part of our lives and which has turned the world upside down so many times.

We are polarised and fulfilled by God in this sexual aspect.

The Christian monks named this love received from God as *Divine Eros.* All those who reached God felt it.

Technically, this is what happens: through love, prayer, spiritual practice, fasting or any other method we choose to reach God.The Kundalini energy, dormant at the base of our spine, awakens and rises. The first Chakra is Muladhara. That is where Kundalini resides. The second one is Swadistana, the erotic centre.

Kundalini arises from centre to centre till the Sahasrara Chakra, where it lives in the happiness of complete union with God. In a spiritually awakened human being, this energy is rising continuously. It is both at the top and at the base. The sky and the earth are united in itself. The energy awakened at the base goes through the second centre, not around it, even though the person has chosen abstinence or celibacy. They will feel a powerful awakening of the erotic energy. Being with heart and mind centred in God, the energy from Swadistana instantly sublimates into the heart chakra, achieving the overwhelming divine love, or into Sahasrara where the feeling of Oneness is experienced.

Practically, this human being will experience orgasms, but not the usual type. These are cosmic orgasms.

What are cosmic orgasms?

The erotic energy that was awakened will conduct an orgasm through the polarisation experienced by the person in his or her relationship with God.

We are permanently polarised by God even if we don't know it.

The energy is not consumed at the level of Swadistana, not lost as it happens in the normal orgasm. It becomes a trampoline, pumping the energy to the higher levels of the being. This is when the person experiences what we might call an orgasm, but it will include all of God's love, as a matter of fact all of the world. The being will enter into divine ecstasy, *Samadhi*.

This happens naturally with someone who has attained union with God.

It is obvious that such a person will never experience sexual frustration.

They will live a cosmic love with the divine lover, God.

I was saying earlier that through the love of God we experience a total fulfilment and we'll never feel the sentiment of lacking. This also include the erotic aspect of our being.

22. The way people approach me is the way I come to them, because people approach me in my ways. – The BhagavadGita

This quote comes as a continuation of the previous subchapter.

Even if it might seem unimaginable to the human mind, God might have another, different role in our life than that of the Father, which is often attributed to Him.

First of all, God has no sex, so he can be a Father or Mother too.

Secondly, the idea that God is our friend started to appear. We have a real example of that in Neale Donald Walsch.

God is complete. He is everything for us. *He* is everything.

You won't open your heart and your soul to Him when you see Him as a Father as you would when you see him as a friend. The father might sometimes reprove you, sometimes he mightpunish you. You may fear Him and you may also feel shy abouttelling Him everything.

Either way, we know that He knows everything about us and there is no hiding place from Him, as David said in the Psalms.

But if we see Him as a Father, we might be shy to tell Him because our mind associates the word 'Father' with the idea of forming a family. He is nurturing us, giving us all we need, even scolding us when we are wrong so, when we feel we have done something that is not right, we will hide.

We won't hide from a friend. We can tell him everything, he is understanding, he shares our emotions and experiences. Thus, by seeing God as our friend, we instantly become closer to Him.

In the same way, we can choose to see Him as our Lover. A real lover is our father, our brother, our husband, our friend and our lover, all at the same time. By choosing Him to be our lover, we are choosing Him to be Everything to us. We are not excluding even one aspect of life in our relationship with Him.

Many Christian saints, and others too, lived this love. If you read Rumi's poems you would think that he was passionately in love with a woman. But the woman he loved was noneotherthan the Divine Lover.

Most peopleclose their minds to the idea of God being our Lover. This is because they associate lovemaking with something despicable and shameful. But if God gifted us with it, why deny it? Many hide theirlovemaking, savouring it yet feeling ashamed. Why is it that this intense pleasure, this joy of the soul that leads us to fulfilment, is associated with the idea of sin? This is one of the big confusions of the human mind. On one hand, the fulfilment they feel is greater than with anythingelse; on the other hand, they refuse to admit this truth. When two human beings truly love each other, this union of their bodies leads to a fulfilment similar to that of the union with God. If the love disappears, the distance from God increases.

Some will say that sexuality's purpose is procreation, to bring a new life tothis world and not pleasure. I'll give you two answers. First is that God has offered us pleasure as a gift, including the sexual aspect(imagine the frustration of being shown a cake and then not being allowed to touch it?). This would be an act of a sadistic God and that could not be further from the truth. God is pure love. The second is that through love, God chose to be born into this world. How beautiful isthe understanding that this love, this fulfilment, can bring a new life.

Returning to the main idea here, what I am trying to emphasise is how, through the love for God, we experience this fulfilment, the erotic one, the feeling that we are His lover.

23. All of us have a relationship with God.

It is just that some of us are more aware of this than others. This relationship with God started at the beginning of time. Many invoke the importance of having a relationship with God, but what they are really saying is that you need *to build that relationship with Him.* We have nothing to build. It already exists and all we need to do is be aware of it.

This is a thing that is done gradually. First, we believe, then see what it consists of and then we observehow such a relationship unfolds.

If in our physical world, in order to start a relationship with someone, we first need their approval, in the relationship with God we already have His approval. We are the only ones needing to approve it.

Then the two would maintain the relationship. How can you maintain a relationship? It needs a phone call, at least now and then, to find out how the other is and an interest inthe other. You do something in order to maintain it and you know that the relationship won't work if you don't do something to keep it going. It's the same with God too. We need to do something in order to keep this relationship. Not just pray. If we only call our friend when we need his help or money or when we are in trouble, how would such a relationship pan out? The friend would have to manifest great love and detachment for us in order to stay in that relationship where we never find the time to visit them, call them or spend time with them. The same is true with our Good God. We need to create time for Him, time that will be dedicated only to Him. To talk to Him, to bring Him gifts, to pay attention to Him out of love and longing and not only when we are in big trouble and we need help.

Our relationship with God is real and it's up to us how we maintain and develop it.

24. God rejoices when we thank Him and not only then.

He rejoices when we offer Him our time, when we talk to Him, when we bring Him gifts and so on.

Got is not dead nor is He absent. He is present and active in our lives. He is living our life together with us. He does everything for us, unconditionally. He is not helping us or covering us with gifts just because we did something to deserve it or in return for our prayers. He is continuously offering us gifts, overwhelming us with His love and attention. That's why He will rejoice if we observe what he does for us and we thank Him, if he feels that we love Him, when attention and gifts are offered to Him, no matter how small they are. From God's perspective, which is beyond duality, there is no small thing or great thing. Feeling the need to give Him something, choosing

213

a gift for Him with all our emotions, that's what matters. Our emotion of offering Him something, the joy that comes with the offering and the love are what matter to Him.

I will give you another example from the Hindu culture because they have understood this aspect: Hindus always go to the temple with offerings that they choose with great care, which are given with great joy. The prayers they make to the deity may also be important and beneficial, but for them, the offering, the gift is very important.

You could ask why would God rejoice in our gifts, our love or our gratitude when he already has all the joy because He is joy Himself?

Because this is how we show Him that we are aware of our relationship with Him, that we haven't forgotten Him. We do this in order to have a conscious relationship with Him.

25. The true meaning of offering.

Offering doesn't just mean bringing flowers, fruits and sweets to the altar. The act of offering has a greater meaning.

In order to be with God all the time, to keep alive this relationship, the best thing is to always be in love with Him.

Whenever we are in love and are starting a relationship with someone, isn't it true that we constantly think about the other? Our soul is full of emotion and we permanently feel that we are in contact with the loved one.

It's the same with God. In order to keep this relationship alive, real and aware, we have to demonstrate that we are always thinking about Him and permanently offering Him gifts. How could we enhance this? By offering ourselves to Him. The supreme offering, the supreme gift is our being. Why would we keep something just for us? Let's give Him everything, all our being, all of our emotions, sentiments, states, thoughts and objects that we might believe belong to us. I say 'believe' because this is what the illusion does, it makes us believe. When we leave this world, there is nothing material that we can take with us. Thus, all that belongs to us, all the material goods, were just offered to us for our use by God Himself. So the best we can do is offer them to Him, together with all that we are.

We can also offer Him all that we do, all our actions. If we are attached to the actions and their results, we are drifting apart from God. Actually, as I've previously said, God does everything together with us so it would be rude on our part to put Him aside and tell Him: *I'll do that*. Or to ignore Him, because He is there anyway, helping us and, most of the time, actually doing things for us.

It would be unjust to cast Him aside and to say that we did it.

Thus, offering our actions means being aware that God is the one doing them through us.

26. With our minds, we are creating universes.

In His love for us, God gave us the freedom not only to choose what to do but to also create the universe in which we live. The mind is the one projecting it. The context of our life appears according to what we think and feel.

It is not an option.

It is a law of the Universe we live in and it is applied no matter whether we know or acknowledge it or not.

In this way, we cannot blame others for the situations in our life. We should know that we are the authors of our life, be it beautiful or tormented.

Yes, it's true. God gave us the freedom to direct our own life.

A thought invested with emotion creates a universe. Any thought and any emotion. It will be a world where we asked to live.

If we don't know the mechanism, we will wake up in a painful situation and we will complain saying: *Who brought me here? Who wishes me ill? It's my genetical inheritance. That's to blame...* etc.

We will always find someone else to blame for the lives we live but it will never be ourselves.

It is even more unjust when we blame God for all that is happening to us. We will then say that He doesn't love us or that He is punishing us or that He doesn't care about us, that we don't deserve His attention or that we are sinners to have a beautiful life.

Thinking like that is very wrong. Everything that happens in our life is our choice and we created it ourselves.

One of the most beautiful graces that God bestowed on us is the ability to build our own life, the life we wish to live.

If one single aspect had been imposed, then yes, we would have a reason to complain, but in His immense love, God respected our freedom completely.

We chose our birth, when and where to come, we chose what to do in life, we are choosing when to get sick and when to recover and even about when we leave this world.

The subject is so broad and may not be that easy to understand. It is explained in greater detail in the course on happiness that I am facilitating.

27. Whoever has will be given more, whoever does not have, even what they have will be taken from them – said our Lord Jesus.

Some might say: *But it is so unfair! Why would the rich ones receive more when they already have everything and why should those who have nothing lose even what they have? Where is the Divine justice here?*

The Divine justice is in our hands. God loves us so much that He won't judge or punish us. As I said before, we choose the good and bad in our lives.

The rich ones are always enjoying what they have and they live in plenitude. They have confidence and they trust that they have enough money and that they can earn more easily. Thinking like this, they are always programming a thriving future.

On the other side, the needy are always complaining about not having enough, about living in poverty and even if they have something, they say that they have nothing. In their self-pity, they are denying even what they do have. That's what they are asking for, that's the program running in their minds. That explains the words of Jesus saying that those who do not have will lose even the little that they have.

So, if we understand this law and we become optimists and enjoy what we have, without thinking that it is little, we will receive more. The more we rejoice, the more we will receive. The secret of an abundant life is in the joy we are experiencing.

This law functions in all the aspects of our life, not only the material one. It works in love, in health, in our work, in spirituality, it works in Everything.

Our future is built on our thoughts and experiences.

28. God always forgives us.

He forgives us as soon as we make a mistake due to His immense kindness. Where would He find space for affronts?

His heart is full of love and forgiveness.

We are the ones unable to forgive and the punishment we assign to God is actually coming from us. We are the ones punishing ourselves because we can't forgive ourselves. Our subconscious is recording and the mind puts labels on what we did: good or bad. Then our soul is the one considering if we deserve the punishment or not. Once we have given ourselves the verdict then the punishment comes when we are ready to atone for it. Even that moment is a choice we make.

God always forgives us.

The hardest thing for us is to forgive ourselves. It's easier to forgive others. Even though we forget what we did, our soul does not forget and awaits the punishment. It will surely come, since it's awaited.

It would be so wonderful if people would forgive-absolve themselves and stop assigning to God all this injustice of saying *I have not been forgiven.*

29. God is happiness.

After we discover God in our hearts, whenever we wake up in the morning or during the night, together with our eyes our heart opens too and the first sensation we feel upon waking up is a wave of immense love flowing over us, encompassing the entire room, the whole house, all the world…and we feel God's love. This love appears just before we are completely awake so our first feeling upon waking up is that of the immensity of God's love. Every day you are waking up in a beautiful world and not in that of suffering.

Even if there won't be any other advantages owing to your relationship with God, this happiness that you feel when you open your eyes is enough to create the desire of completely surrendering yourself to Him.

God is in our heart and thus, in our heart resides the source of the total, unconditional happiness.

Part IV

METHODS AND MEDITATIONS

JOURNAL

I arrived at this point of writing the book and again, I stopped. I knew many would be troubled and I had to choose either to continue or to stop and keep all the experiences and revelations just for myself.

As I said, we have a guesthouse in the mountains where it's usual for spiritual groups to come and hold camps. It's a remote place in a scenic spot and some say that they can feel a special spiritual field.

We didn't make a fuss about this. We rented the guesthouse to anyone who wanted to come, no matter if it was for a spiritual camp, a school camp or parties. The guesthouse is our source of income.

The leader of one of the groups coming to our guesthouse for years now, is supposed to be a visionary. We offer discretion to all of our guests. They rent the guesthouse and we are not interested in their activities, and we don't disturb them. I never spoke to the man who was called a visionary by the others. Only my husband did and just on logistic matters.

Now, at this point of my writing, we exchanged a few words. It was the end of a camp and he didn't have that much time, needing to return home. We settled that in two weeks' time, when he would return, he would remain for a day more just so we would be able to talk.

That day came and all four of us had a conversation: my husband and I, he and his wife.

Each time he would say something, his wife would look at him with admiration and respect. She was sure that everythinghe said was true. I still didn't know them.

We talked for a few hours. At first, everything seemed foggy. I was not able to understand the things he was saying. Gradually everythingcame to light and I started to understand.

- What's up with you, what is bothering you?*he asked me.*

I told him that I am writing a book and something is not letting me finish it. Then I told him what was holding me back, without telling him what the book wasabout.

With discretion and diplomacy, he performedhis mission, stimulating me to go ahead. He was not talking about the book but about some aspects related to me, my incarnation and my mission on earth.

As we talked, I understood more about the events in my life.

Bythe end of our conversation I was able to understand a lot and I felt ready to continue writing the book and publishing it.

In the end he said:

- Finish the book – *even though he didn't know what the book was about.*

So here I write again.

I will tell you now about a few methods that are useful on our path to God.

1. Food offering

I have already talked about God's joy on receiving gifts from us.

Now we will talkabout God being everywhere, in all there is, even in us and in our hearts. We mentioned that God is always with us and it would be rude on our part to ignore His presence.

The method I will tell you about is related to the transformation of the food we eat every day in an offering that we will give to God who resides within us.

Thus, the feeding process becomes sacred and the food will have a different value.

On the other side, we are permanently aware of the presence of God in our beings.

Whenever we cook, we should think we are preparing the food for God Himself. No matter if we eat it or not, God is also in all the other people, so we are still cooking for Him.

Then, as we serve it to the others, we can say in our mind:

Lord, please receive this offering that I prepared for you with so much love.

When the offering is received in this way, God, residing in the others, will be the one consuming that food. Through this simple method, in time, those people will become aware of the God living in them.

If we are the ones to consume it, we should say the same, this time paying attention to how God, in us, is receiving that food.

I've undertaken this exercise with my students at seminars and each of us had pleasant surprises. Here are a few testimonials:

- *I felt how the food was transforming into energy and how it was nourishing every cell and atom in my being.*
- *I felt the food transforming into light that was then shining through my entire body.*
- *I was not feeling hungry and I was a little shy at first, seeing that you've brought food for us. As I started to swallow, I felt that an immense stomach had opened inside me where any amount of food would have entered. It was clear to me that God received the offering.*
- *I was feeling the food till it reached my throat and then it transformed into pure energy.*
- *As I was eating the food, I felt delicate and refined vibrations spreading through my body to its extremities.*
- *I felt that all my subtle bodies were nourished and not just my physical body.*

So, through this manner of feeding ourselves and the attitude we have towards food, we become more aware of what is going on with us when we are eating and, even more, through the offering that is then received by God. The food then becomes purer and the feeding process becomes sacred.

This is a method of deification: offering the food to God, in us, we will discover Him even more until He will be completely revealed.

The food transforms into *amrita*, the divine nectar, which will offer us immortality, in return.

2. The method of forgiveness – 1

I kept asking myself how it was possible for some saints or priests to tell the people who made mistakes: *You can now leave, you have been forgiven.*

I wanted to understand who gave them the right to forgive when, as per my understanding, only God had that power. Maybe the priests receive a certain investiture, but in my mind, something didn't make sense.

As I said before, God is present in our lives and grants all our wishes so that cleared how it is that some people can offer His forgiveness.

I was offered this teaching through an exemplification:

I was really upset withsomeone, so upset that I would have never forgiven them. But I was in that phase where I kept asking questions about forgiveness. Unexpectedly, because I was active and not meditating or praying, I felt Jesus' presence and then I felt Him entering into my being through the top of my head. Once He encompassed me completely and I felt I was one with Him, I perceived Him forgiving that person. Jesus forgave him. I was witnessing it both from the inside and from the outside, as I was at once both One with Jesus and a witness to what was happening. I immediately felt that all the karma relating to that event had disappeared. I felt no trace of judgment from Jesus in this act of forgiveness that He undertook, no remorse towards the one I was upset with, nor towards me for losing my temper. Jesus manifested immense love that was completely detached, as well as an incomparable kindness.

On this occasion, I understood how the forgiveness instantly dissolved the karma. Just through the process of forgiveness, we can get rid of all the karma that we are carrying. That's why it is so important to forgive – in this way we are erasing a consequence that might have followed.

The moment of my union with Christ and of the forgiveness was very beautiful and it is difficult to express it through words.

Once the amazement subsided,I gathered all the pieces and I understood the method and the answer I was searching for.

All those saints were justified in giving forgiveness because they were permanently one with Jesus (the Christian ones) or with God (the ones of other faiths).

They were aware of that state and they were, in fact, offering God's forgiveness, because God was in them. In order to do that you really need to be one with God and be aware of that.

I understood that it could become a method, I practiced it on other occasions and it worked. Together with the forgiveness that Jesus offered, the karma related to the event disappeared. This can be easily observed through what you feel towards that person. When you are involved and there is karma, you feel anger, dismay, frustration, etc. Once that person is forgiven what follows is a state of complete detachment. The negative states won't transform into positive ones (love, reconciliation, tolerance, etc.) because as long as there are states, no matter whether they are good ones or bad ones, there is also a karma that ties you to it. It simply remains a complete detachment that doesn't trouble you when you think of that person or event. But it is important not to mistake detachment with indifference, so beware.

Here are the steps:

- Find a quiet place where you won't be disturbed.
- You may stand up, sit on a chair or in a meditation posture. Don't do this lying down under any circumstances, so that you donot fall asleep.
- We will offer to God this action and we'll transform into offerings all that we are doing, even this method.
- We relax, forgetting about all other concerns unrelated to the event we wish to forgive.
- We will evoke Jesus and we will pray to Him to come to us. We will wait until His presence is felt. Don't think that He won't come or that you are too small to get His attention or that you don't deserve the grace of His presence. He is one with the Father so He has all the qualities of the Father:

love, compassion, forgiveness, desire to help and so on. If we are calling Him with faith and sincere love, He will certainly come.

- Once He comes, we will ask Him to enter our being. He will enter through the top of our head and we will feel our being embraced by Him. We will also experience the special joy of the union with Him.
- We will then ask Him to forgive… (we will clearly say the name of the person who wronged us) and we will have a clear idea in our minds about the situation.
- We will wait patiently, paying attention to what is happening. From here on, Jesus does all the work. He will forgive. Maybe we are not able to forgive yet, but if we release this into God's hands, he will do it.
- Together with the feeling of forgiveness, we will feel how the karmic tie is broken and the situation disappears from our aura.
- At the end, it is important to show our gratitude for all that we have experienced.

3. The method of forgiveness – 2

We have learned one method of how to forgive above, but forgiveness has two faces: to forgive and to be forgiven. We must have surely made many mistakes, with or without our knowledge or will and we must have upset some people in our life. Now is the moment to ask for forgiveness.

How do we do that?

Once again, we will start from the Truth that God resides in each of us.

It might be possible that in some cases we won't have the ability to ask for forgiveness in person because the person we wronged has moved to a different place and we have lost contact with them or maybe they have passed away. This doesn't mean that there is no more karma there. Our soul remembers everything. Sometimes, the guilt haunts us and we are tormented because we haven't got access to the person we want to ask for forgiveness.

It's easier when the person is nearby. We ask for their forgiveness, we reconcile and the situation is sorted.

But what if they don't want to forgive us or if they don't want to talk to us?

Then our soul will carry the burden of karma, whether we are aware of it or not.

With all the events that crowd our life, it is difficult to remember everything that has happened. Sometimes we make mistakes without realising it. We are moving on, but the soul has recorded the pain we inflicted. The soul does not forget.

For these situations, there is a very simple method.

Here are the steps:

- Find a quiet place where you won't be disturbed.
- We will offer to God the action of realising this method.
- We relax.
- We clear our minds of all other thoughts unrelated to our purpose (the situation, the person and the intention to ask for forgiveness).
- We clearly bring to our mind the situation when we did wrong.
- We visualise clearly the person to whom we did wrong.
- We look at her/him with detachment.
- We remember the Truth that God is in every being, thus He is in us and in the person in front of us.
- We will try to 'see' and feel God in that person. We stay where we are till we are able to do that.
- We will ask for forgiveness to God in that being. God is always forgiving so we will surely be forgiven
- After we receive forgiveness, we will try to feel the state that is appearing within us and towards that person (will it be love, reconciliation, the need to embrace them). We will perform this gesture in our mind, knowing that their soul will receive it.
- We then thank God who is in us and in that person.

The karma will be broken and our soul will be released from the mistake we made in the past if the method was successful.

All we have to do is perform it.

No matter who our God is, no matter what the spiritual path we are on or our religion, both methods can be used by connecting ourselves with the God we believe in.

4. A simple method to converse with God

As I was saying, a relationship needs attention in order to grow. People usually go to God when they are in need or in trouble.

To converse with God is a great advantage to us and a great joy for God. Why? It's simple. Because we are not ignoring Him. It's a way to show Him that He is of interest to us.

If we are able to really converse with Him, and not just in our imagination, we can ask for advice whenever we might need it. Who would be more entitled to advise us than Him?

We can receive advice from Him when we need to make a decision. We can receive teachings and advice directly from Him, since He is the Great Teacher. We can ask him directly to give us something when we need it and we will know he has heard us. By using a prayer, some would be wondering whether he heard it or not. When we converse with Him, we are sure that He did hear it.

I'm sure you sense there are many other advantages of conversing with Him beyond what I've just outlined.

Now let's demolish this idea that we can't converse with Him (because He is too far and He won't be able to hear us, He is too busy with something else, we are not important to Him, He won't answer us, we don't deserve His attention and so on). All these or other ideas that might go through the mind of a sceptical person are simply not true.

God is always with us, He is closer to us than we can imagine, He is always watching over us, He always wants us to be good and happy, we have all His attention and He is always answering us. We barely have the chance to utter the question and He will immediately give us the answer. He is answering us directly, rapidly and without messengers. It's just that we often can't hear Him because of lack of confidence, because we don't know we can converse with Him or because we haven't developed our subtle hearing

Lately, this belief that God is answering us is more visible. We believe that He is answering us through signs, through messages we've seen on some poster, through the people passing by and telling someone else something that was destined for us or by opening a special book, etc.

With a little courage, faith and trust, each of us can converse with God.

How can we do that?

It's simple. First find a place where you won't be disturbed. A quiet place, maybe at night when all the others are sleeping. Shut off all TVs, radios, CD players, phones, etc. In total silence, call God. He is there already, but through this calling you become aware of His presence. Then talk to Him. Not too much, because He knows everything about you. Talk to Him as much as you need to, till you feel you have established contact with Him. For example, you can tell Him how your day was. Or tell Him what impressed you. Or you can talk to Him about someone. It's just an introduction. Speak slowly, with no rush. Then, if you have a dilemma or a decision to make, ask Him: *What do You say, my Lord, what should I do in this situation?*

You will need to stop then. He will answer straight away because He needs no time to think.

If you don't stop talking and your mind is continuously agitated, you will notbe able to hear Him.

If you are quiet you will hear His answer. It will surprise you. This is proof that the answer is coming from Him and it's not your mind playing tricks on you. When your imagination is playing with you and you believe that God answered when in fact it was you, the answer is usually something that you were expecting. When it comes from Him, you will shudder. Most of the time, the answer doesn't please the ego. It seems hard to follow, to apply. Each time, the answer is unexpected.

Anyone can talk to God. God is there for all of us.

All we need is faith and practice.

5. One hour with God

The most important meditation (I'm calling it that for convenience, but it's not necessarily a meditation) isto spend one hour each day with God. If we usually meditate, we can adopt a comfortable position or a meditation asana and focus our mind and heart on God. We are simply there with Him. We offer Him an hour out of the twenty-four hours He gave us each day- an hour when we are not praying for anything, when we are not asking for anything. All we are doing is thinking of Him.

Shortly, we will see surprising results.

If we don't know how to meditate and we have another spiritual orientation, Christian or of any other nature, we can kneel or sit on a chair for an hour, but never lie on the ground or on the bed because we might fall asleep.

It doesn't matter what name we give to God; as long as we are offering an hour of our life each day to Him, He will be grateful.

JOURNAL

I said that there was once a moment in my life when someone left me and, because of that, I was feeling lost and I oriented all my attention to Jesus. A series of spiritual experiences, lessons and realisations followed, determining the spectre of this book.

The person I am referring to was so upset with me, that for years he did not want to talk to me again. Meanwhile, my soul was cured, but I still had a little regret that he would never know the good that his leaving brought to my life.

After I wrote the last chapter of this book, I sighed with relief and enjoyed the feeling of completing it.

One hour later, surprise! That person contacted me, first online and then on the phone. I was amazed because we had never spoken since he left. We reconciled and we forgave each other joyously.

Some modern spiritual trends use the expression – the circle was closed.

That happened in this case also: this person who determined the course of this spiritual adventure, ending with the writing of this book, reappeared exactly when I had finished what I had to do.

What can I say? That the circle was closed or that this person played an important part, was a divine instrument, in the transmission of these messages from God, through this book?

Indeed, mysterious are the paths of God.

ABANDON YOURSELVES
AND LET GOD MAKE YOU HAPPY!

www.ingramcontent.com/pod-product-compliance
Lightning Source LLC
Chambersburg PA
CBHW030837300326
41935CB00037B/486